Made Known to Them

Made Known to Them

An Invitation to the Study of Theology

Douglas M. Koskela

CASCADE *Books* • Eugene, Oregon

MADE KNOWN TO THEM
An Invitation to the Study of Theology

Cascade Books
An Imprint of Wipf and Stock Publishers
199 W. 8th Ave., Suite 3
Eugene, OR 97401

www.wipfandstock.com

PAPERBACK ISBN: 979-8-3852-0199-0
HARDCOVER ISBN: 979-8-3852-0200-3
EBOOK ISBN: 979-8-3852-0201-0

Cataloguing-in-Publication data:

Names: Koskela, Douglas M., author.

Title: Made known to them : an invitation to the study of theology / by Douglas M. Koskela.

Description: Eugene, OR : Cascade Books, 2025 | Includes bibliographical references.

Identifiers: ISBN 979-8-3852-0199-0 (paperback) | ISBN 979-8-3852-0200-3 (hardcover) | ISBN 979-8-3852-0201-0 (ebook)

Subjects: LCSH: Theology. | Bible—Meditations.

Classification: BR118 .K67 2025 (paperback) | BR118 .K67 (ebook)

VERSION NUMBER 06/24/25

Dedicated to the memory of three who
walked along the road with me:

William J. Abraham
(1947–2021)

Roger A. Koskela
(1938–2024)

C. Edward Smyth
(1943–2024)

Contents

Preface

As its subtitle suggests, this book is an invitation. You are invited to join countless others across the centuries who have taken up the study of Christian theology. Many of us who love this work find not only that it stirs our intellect but also that it touches something deeper in our souls. If you have ever realized how much you had been craving a certain food only after you started eating it, or realized how much you wanted to hear a certain song only after it started playing, theology can be something like that. Students often find that this is a subject that begins to address questions they didn't fully realize their souls were asking. At its most basic, theology is the study of God and what God has done. And so the hunger that theology taps into is our deep hunger for God. Christians across the ages have insisted that we were made by God and for God; that he alone can truly make us happy in the long run. If they are right about that, then this is surely a hunger worth feeding.

We should be clear at that outset that this is not an introduction to the *content* of Christian theology. If you are reading this book as part of an introductory class in theology, you will have other texts and lectures to acquaint you with the basics of Christian teaching. This book is rather an opportunity for us to think together about what the study of theology involves and how we can best go about it. It offers a number of important things to keep in mind as you proceed. In that respect, it may be worth holding onto this book and coming back to it occasionally throughout the course of your studies in theology. Some of the things that we understand so clearly in the early stages of a journey become muddled or forgotten down the road, and often these are the very things that might help orient us in more difficult stages of travel.

That image of a journey is a helpful one in the study of Christian theology. And in this book, we will organize our reflections around a biblical story about a journey. The story is found in Luke 24:13–35. This is a passage about two disciples of Jesus who are walking down a road to a village called Emmaus. It is set on the morning of Jesus's resurrection, and while the disciples have heard a report that Jesus's tomb is empty, they do not yet know whether to believe it. As they walk, a mysterious stranger comes alongside them and engages them in conversation. We, the readers, are told that this stranger is the risen Jesus himself, but the disciples in the story do not yet realize it. In the course of this story, we find many pointers to what faithful theology should look like. Each chapter of this book will explore one of those aspects of theology, along with reflections on the particular moment in the Emmaus narrative that signals it.

This way of approaching our topic will hopefully begin to give you a sense—or deepen your sense—of the inexhaustible richness of Scripture. The Bible is full of stories like this; stories that can transform us precisely as we read about the change that God brings about in the lives of the people in them. With that in mind, I might encourage you to do two things as you read this book. First, each time you sit down to read a portion of this book, re-read the Emmaus passage in the Gospel of Luke before you begin. Having the whole story in mind is helpful as we consider specific parts of it. But even more, the careful and repeated reading of a particular passage of Scripture can begin to yield more and more treasures over time. Second, I would invite you to pray each time you begin to read this book. Ask that God would draw you to himself through the course of your studies. As I will say repeatedly in the pages that follow, that, more than anything else, is what we are seeking in theology. I should mention that, while working on this book, I did those two things each time I sat down to write.

I found them helpful practices in reminding myself of the very purpose of theological study.

As I hinted at the outset, this is mainly a book for beginners. I suspect that it will primarily be used in introductory theology classes or given as a gift to those starting a seminary program or an undergraduate theology program. But it is not only a book for beginners. Those of us who have been at this for a while may well find these reminders about the nature of theology to be helpful. Sometimes those with the firmest grasp of the content of Christian teaching can find it most challenging to reconnect with the ultimate aim of our calling. In such cases, my hope is that these signposts in the Emmaus story can be useful to that end. It is a wonderful gift to be able to study the nature and activity of the living God, and I trust a sense of that will come through in these pages.

So now I invite you to set out on your journey. The disciples in the Emmaus story shared a walk, a meal, and ultimately the company of other disciples of Jesus when they returned to Jerusalem. Along the way, they experienced conversations about Scripture that made their hearts burn within them. They were enabled to see what they could not see before. And they found themselves in the company of the God who has made himself known in Jesus. I am confident that similar things await you on the path ahead. In that light, this is indeed a journey worth taking.

Chapter 1: The Report from the Tomb

THE EMMAUS STORY IN Luke 24 begins with a conversation between two people on a journey. They are talking, we read, about "all these things that had happened" (v. 14).[1] When a stranger walks up and joins the conversation, he asks the question that opens the door to further details: "What things?" The two travelers reply that they are talking about recent events in Jerusalem concerning Jesus of Nazareth—the very person, they will later realize, who has joined them along the road. One of the travelers, named Cleopas, implies that just about everyone in Jerusalem has been talking about these things since the crucifixion of Jesus a few days earlier. Yet for these two, there is a new energy in the conversation on this particular day.

The reason for this intensity emerges in verses 22–24. Some women among Jesus's disciples had gone to the tomb early that morning and had found it empty. They reported that they had seen a vision of angels who said that Jesus was alive. When some of those disciples who heard the women's testimony went to the tomb themselves, they found it just as the women had said. Of course, readers of Luke's Gospel already know this part of the story, as it is narrated in the first twelve verses of chapter 24. But now the women's testimony of the empty tomb and of the angels' words animates the conversation on the road to Emmaus.

---

1. All biblical quotations are taken from the New Revised Standard Version (NRSV).

1

This book is an invitation to the study of theology. As we might expect, the study of theology involves a great deal of reading, writing, and conversation. But we will see that it also includes prayer, worship, attentiveness, and reflection. In what follows, we will learn more about what the work of theology involves by meditating on the Emmaus story. Each chapter will take a cue from something that happens in that narrative. And our first observation is precisely the women's testimony that has "astounded" the disciples on the way to Emmaus. This moment in the story signals an important starting point: *Christian theology begins with testimony to God's action.*

The angels at the tomb have proclaimed that Jesus is alive, and the women report that astounding news to the other disciples. It is true that, at least in the way that Luke's Gospel narrates the story, the women have not yet seen the risen Jesus. And it is also true that many of the disciples who hear the women's claims do not believe them. This even seems to include Cleopas and his traveling companion, if we are to make sense of the reprimand they receive from Jesus in verse 25. But the point still stands that testimony to the resurrection of Jesus drives the energy of the conversation on the Emmaus road. The two disciples are astounded by the report of the empty tomb and the angels, and they are trying to make sense of it when Jesus joins them.

I want to suggest that this feature of the Emmaus story is an important signpost for us in thinking about the nature of theology. A good way to understand the work of Christian theology is disciplined, prayerful reflection on the activity of God for the redemption of the world. This activity is centered in the incarnation, death, and resurrection of Jesus. Those who take up the study of theology aim to consider what these actions of God suggest about the nature of God, the nature of creation and human beings, and the relationship between them. The invitation to theological study, then, first comes though the announcement of these saving actions of God. To put the matter a bit differently, what comes first is the proclamation of the gospel—that is, the good news of salvation through the redemptive actions of God in

Jesus. The particular work of theology in response to that proclamation is to explore what those divine actions suggest about God, about us, and about the world we live in.

To be sure, our own experiences and questions will play an important role in the work of theology once we get started. But it is vitally important for us to recognize that those experiences and questions are not the starting point for authentically Christian theology. The testimony to particular actions of God, by an actual community of people across the generations, is where the work of theology begins. It emerges from an encounter with the claim that *God has done something* very specific. It is true, of course, that our own ponderings about the origin of the universe or the meaning of life might precede an actual encounter with the gospel. But only when we are confronted with the announcement that "in Christ God was reconciling the world to himself" (2 Cor 5:19) do those philosophical musings lead us to Christian theology proper.

When we get this ordering right, we will find along the way many contact points to our prior experiences and questions. Many people who have come to Christian faith found that much in their lives before was pointing them toward the God who is revealed in Jesus. But it is the proclamation of the gospel, and all that follows as we respond, that helps us to make sense of that prior experience. We do not extrapolate from our own musings on our experience to learn who God is and what he has done. Rather, we hear testimony of God's actions in Jesus, and that opens the door to a lifelong process of response. Drawing nearer and nearer to that God with our hearts, wills, and minds, we gradually come to see ourselves and our world more clearly in light of their relation to God. But this can really only happen if the revelatory actions of God—and not our own experiences—provide the raw material of theological reflection.

One of the clearest places in the New Testament where we see these dynamics at work is the book of Acts. Written by the same author as the Gospel of Luke, Acts tells the story of the community of Jesus's disciples after the resurrection and ascension of Jesus. In many respects, the church is born when the Holy Spirit fills and empowers these disciples on the day of Pentecost, which we read about in Acts 2. But before that pivotal event, we read in Acts 1 the last words that Jesus tells the apostles before his ascension: "You will receive power when the Holy Spirit has come upon you, and you will be my witnesses in Jerusalem, in all Judea and Samaria, and to the ends of the earth" (1:8).

The specific nature of the testimony that these apostles will bring to the ends of the earth becomes even clearer later in the chapter. After the apostles had returned to Jerusalem and joined the larger group of disciples in an ongoing habit of prayer, Peter addresses the crowd. He suggests that the place of Judas among the apostles must be filled in the wake of Judas's betrayal of Jesus. "One of the men who have accompanied us during all the time that the Lord Jesus went in and out among us," Peter contends, "one of these must become a witness with us to his resurrection" (1:21–22). It is important for us to pay close attention to that last phrase. The apostles are charged to be witnesses to Jesus through-out the entire world, and specifically they are to be witnesses *to the resurrection*. The proper work of this Apostolic community is to witness to the specific acts of God in Jesus—culminating in Jesus's resurrection—for the salvation of the world.

As we read through the rest of the book of Acts, this is pre-cisely what the apostles do. Immediately after the experience at Pentecost, for example, Peter speaks to the crowd that had gathered in response. He testifies to the resurrection of Jesus (2:24, 32) and indicates that God's action had enabled their salvation (2:21, cit-ing a passage from the book of Joel, and 2:38–40). Peter continues this pattern in chapter 3, in his speech at Solomon's Portico. There he proclaims the resurrection of Jesus, with the emphatic echo of his earlier statement from chapter 1: "To this we are witnesses" (3:15). This culminates in a call to salvation in 3:19–26. And again in chapter 4, Peter addresses a who's who of religious leadership in Jerusalem. Filled with the Holy Spirit, he testifies to the resur-rection of Jesus (4:10) and claims unequivocally that salvation can come through no one else (4:12).

While Peter is at the center of the apostles' witness in these early chapters of Acts, other representatives of the community soon join in this work. Eventually, the apostles begin to expand the geographical scope of their witness, as Jesus had indicated they would. In many of these cases, they find people who already have had significant and genuine experiences of God. We find interesting examples of this in the stories of the Ethiopian court official in Acts 8, the gentile Cornelius and his companions in Acts 10, and Lydia in Acts 16. In each of these narratives, prior experiences of seeking and experiencing God have led these people to hear and respond to the proclamation of the gospel. It is the witness to the saving acts of God in Jesus that makes sense of their prior experiences, and not the other way around.

Perhaps the most striking case is in Acts 17, where Paul is in the city of Athens. While walking through the city, Paul is deeply distressed at the idols he finds around every corner. There are clearly religious instincts among the residents of Athens, but he sees that they are directed toward false gods. When Paul has the opportunity to speak to them, he uses their spirituality as a rhetorical starting point: "Athenians, I see how extremely spiritual you are in every way. For as I went through the city and looked carefully at the objects of your worship, I found among them an altar with the inscription, 'To an unknown god.' What therefore you worship as unknown, this I proclaim to you" (17:22–23). He proceeds to tell the crowd about the God who created everything and who transcends the shrines and idols that are all over the city. Precisely because of God's transcendence, Paul suggests, we find that He is surprisingly close to us all: "In him we live and move and have our being" (17:28).

Paul's remarkable speech to the Athenians culminates in the proclamation of Jesus's resurrection (17:31). And as we might expect, this is precisely the point that intrigues some and repels others. "When they heard of the resurrection of the dead," we read in 17:32, "some scoffed, but others said, 'We will hear you again about this.'" Some of the people who heard that speech become believers, as we learn in verse 34. And it is precisely here that we see our claim at work, that Christian theology begins with testimony to God's action. Paul did not dismiss the religious instincts of the people of Athens, but he did recognize that those instincts were leading them toward a false understanding of God apart from Christ. He took their spirituality as a starting point. But he aimed to guide all of that religious energy toward truth about God by testifying to the particular actions of God in Christ.

We have seen, then, that the proclamation of the gospel is the starting point for theology. But we should also be clear that theology is not the same thing as evangelism. Admittedly, there is no doubt that Paul engages in some rudimentary theology with the Athenians to serve his primary task of sharing the gospel. He insists that the God who created the world transcends the world (Acts 17:24). He makes it clear that mortal creatures receive life and breath as a gift from God, who is perfectly sufficient and needs nothing (17:25). He tells the Athenians that God desires his creatures to seek out a relationship with him, and that God's continual nearness to us makes that possible (17:27–28). And all of this enables Paul to speak of particular actions of God, most specifically the resurrection of Jesus and the coming judgment (17:30–31). In this light, a number of basic theological claims are made in order to proclaim the good news and call the Athenians to repentance.

Still, the activities of evangelism and theology are distinct. We might think of the basic difference between them in this way: evangelism is a first-order activity of proclaiming what God has done for our salvation and inviting people to respond in the power of the Holy Spirit. Theology is a second-order activity of reflecting on who that God is and how these particular actions of God have made possible the redemption of creation. Or we might consider the primary subject matter of each task. The main subject of evangelism is the gospel, the good news that in the incarnation, death, and resurrection of Jesus, God has acted to rescue the world from its slide into chaos and nonbeing. By contrast, the main subject matter of theology is doctrine. The word doctrine simply means teaching, and in the case of Christian theology, it means the teaching of the Christian faith about God, creation, salvation, the church, and the future.

The language of "first-order" and "second-order" above is meant to indicate the idea that the body of Christian doctrine serves to make sense of the basic claims of the gospel. When people respond to the proclamation of the gospel through repentance, conversion, and immersion into the life of the church, certain questions will inevitably arise. If Jesus is truly God, and if Jesus is distinct from God the Father, then do we worship two Gods? If the Holy Spirit is God at work within us and in the world around us, then do we worship three Gods? And if God has acted to save us, what have we been saved from? And so on. If we look at the very first centuries of the Christian church's history, we see a body of teaching begin to emerge in response to these questions.

This body of doctrine was forged through prayerful reflection on the Scriptures and (often very intense) conversation and debate. Sometimes a particular idea would gain traction during these centuries because it offered a clear and simple response to a pressing question—only to be later rejected as false and dangerously misleading. These teachings, known as heresies, were not spurned because the leaders of the church were afraid of a diversity of ideas or intellectual exchange. On the contrary, it was typically vigorous intellectual engagement that led to the rejection of particular heresies. These ideas were dismissed, rather, because they were found to lead people away from a healthy relationship with the God who has acted to save them. The conviction underlying all of this is that false ideas about God and salvation can do genuine spiritual damage.

The body of Christian teaching that emerged in this period came to be reflected in a number of places. We see it in the church's liturgies and prayers; we see it in sermons, commentaries, and other writings; and we see it perhaps most clearly in statements of faith such as creeds. Often these materials came to reflect greater and greater specificity over time as new questions were addressed. For example, the first version of the Nicene Creed came out of the First Ecumenical Council of Nicea (hence the name) in AD

325. An expanded version, and the one we generally know today, emerged from the Council of Constantinople in AD 381. This expanded version included a good deal more about the person and work of the Holy Spirit, reflecting the prayerful discernment of the church on the doctrine of the Holy Spirit over the course of the fourth century.

Another example would be the greater clarity about the person of Jesus that took shape in the following century. After the clear affirmation in the Nicene Creed that Jesus is truly and fully God, new questions were raised about the relationship between Jesus's divine and human natures. The Ecumenical Councils of Ephesus (AD 431) and Chalcedon (AD 451) took up these questions, again in response to ideas that were gaining popularity in some corners of the church. The Definition of Chalcedon that emerged from the latter council rejected these ideas and clarified basic convictions about the two natures of Jesus that would mark Christian teaching from then on.

The Definition of Chalcedon is, in fact, an especially interesting example when it comes to our question of the nature of theology. This is because that statement does not really articulate a detailed Christology; that is, a systematic account of the person and work of Jesus. Rather, what we see in that Definition is the identification of the ground rules that would shape faithful Christology in the life of the church. The statement left plenty of space for various ways of articulating who Jesus is, all of which could be evaluated on their relative merits. But it clearly specified particular boundaries of Christian teaching about Jesus; namely, that Jesus's divine and human natures should be affirmed without confusing, changing, or dividing those two natures.[2] In this light, the Definition of Chalcedon did not close the door on the ongoing work of theology within the church's life. On the contrary, it articulated how genuinely Christian theology might be identified.

Let's now take stock of what we've considered thus far. The Christian faith arose in response to particular actions of God, centered in the incarnation, death, and resurrection of Jesus. (It is

---

2. Leith, *Creeds of the Churches*, 36.

important to note that the stage for these actions of God was set in the story of Israel, as we will explore in chapter 3. So the Christian faith certainly did not emerge out of thin air; it arose in response to divine activity that was understood as part of Israel's particular story.) At the command of Jesus and in the power of the Holy Spirit, the apostolic community set out to testify to these actions of God and invite people to respond. Over time, this church prayerfully cultivated a body of teaching about God and what God has done. This collection of doctrines helped make intellectual sense of the gospel that the church continued (and continues) to proclaim in every generation. This teaching also guided people as they sought to grow closer to the God who had made himself known in Jesus. The ongoing work of theology, then, involves careful reflection on these doctrines about God and God's saving actions in Jesus.

Since this book is an invitation to the study of theology, this brings us to you. You are welcome to enter into this world at any time, wherever you may be on your own journey. But *how* you enter the world of Christian theology will depend on the stage in which you find yourself. Some people begin to reflect on Christian claims about God as they are first hearing the gospel and considering how they will respond. Remember the Athenians of Acts 17, who were in precisely this position. Others may begin a bit further down the road. That is, some people begin to engage in the work of theology after—in some cases long after—they have embraced Christian faith. Often this happens because a Christian wants to know how to go deeper in this faith and is looking for company in that process. In other instances, it begins because someone is feeling intellectually unsettled and wants to explore whether Christianity holds together under scrutiny. Or it may be that someone is feeling called by God to a particular ministry in the church and senses the need for further training in order to obey that call.

From any of these starting points, the journey will need to proceed through some particular waypoints if we are to be faithful in our theological work. It is important to note at the outset, for example, that Christian theology is done from a posture of commitment to Christian faith. This is not by any means to say that one cannot learn or explore the teachings of the Christian faith before becoming a Christian—that is, in fact, a natural part of the process of conversion. But actively entering into the ongoing dialogue of Christian theology requires that one has crossed the threshold of faith. Geoffrey Wainwright put this beautifully in the Preface to his book *For Our Salvation*. He suggested that he was writing "from faith to faith: the reality of the gospel and the truths of Christian doctrine are taken for granted by the author and among the audience."[3] This is an echo of the famous phrase of St. Anselm of Canterbury, who described the work of theology as "faith seeking understanding." There certainly are other kinds of inquiry that involve the rigorous exploration of Christian teaching without any assumption of a faith commitment. The interchange between those outside the faith asking hard questions about Christian doctrine and those who respond is usually called apologetics. And purely descriptive or critical accounts of Christian faith, including its teaching, are offered from a variety of angles in the broad domain of religious studies. But theology proper involves rigorous intellectual exchange among those who embrace the doctrines under consideration.

We should pause here to consider a very natural question that might be raised at this point. If we took as our starting point the testimony to the resurrection in the Emmaus story, then what do we make of the two disciples' seeming unbelief? If this biblical text is to serve as an invitation to theology, how do we understand the fact that the main characters were chastised by Jesus as "foolish" and "slow of heart to believe?" Three things need to be said in response. First, the Emmaus story begins as these very events are unfolding. Cleopas and the other disciple are traveling on the day of Jesus's resurrection, and they have not yet encountered anyone who has seen Jesus with their own eyes. Second, despite their hesitation to believe the testimony they have heard, they are already committed disciples of Jesus. Verse 13 identifies these characters as "two of them," and the antecedent of "them" appears to be "the eleven and . . . all the rest" from verse 9. They have remained in

3. Wainwright, *For Our Salvation*, ix.

company with the apostles and the other disciples. Third, and most important, these travelers do not really know what to do with the women's testimony until Jesus comes among them and begins to dispel their unbelief. We will explore these dynamics more in the chapters to come. For now, it's enough to recognize that these disciples' commitment to Jesus takes clearer shape as these events unfold. And that clarity comes through attentiveness to the Scriptures and table fellowship in the very presence of Jesus.

A second waypoint on the journey of theology is a basic familiarity with Christian doctrine. In order to enter into any conversation, we need to know what has been said so far. And in the case of Christian theology, that will require a basic understanding of the church's teaching. This basic instruction in the faith is often called catechesis. Classically, catechesis was part of the initiation process into the church. One was taught, and demonstrated familiarity with, the central aspects of the Christian faith before one was baptized or confirmed. Ideally, the initiation process for new Christians still works this way. But the reality is that catechesis nowadays is often rather thin or even nonexistent. People can identify as Christians and be active members of a church for a long time with a poor grasp of basic Christian teaching.

My main aim in making this point is not to scold church leaders (or church members, for that matter) for this deficiency in basic instruction. It is to say that some brushing up will need to be done. And thankfully, there are any number of good ways of doing this. If you are starting a program in theology at a college or a seminary, introductory courses nowadays generally do a very good job of filling in gaps in catechesis. If you are in a church setting, there are numerous possibilities for classes or book groups aimed at the basics. Most pastors would be thrilled to hear from church members who are seeking opportunities to learn more about their faith. While many programs in basic Christian doctrine will use only contemporary resources, it is a very good idea to include some classical texts as well. These works have stood the test of time not only because they reflect Christian teaching faithfully, but also because they often are written with a clarity and beauty that is lacking in more recent works.[4]

It is crucial to have a grasp of the basics before going deeper in theology. As we noted above, doctrines are the main subject matter of Christian theology. It is nearly impossible to reflect thoughtfully and fruitfully on the church's teaching without a solid grounding in that teaching. Without a doubt, theology involves more than simply learning and repeating those doctrines. There will be plenty of room down the road for creative and constructive work within the terrain set out by Christian teaching. In fact, much of the real joy and excitement of theology comes in encountering such work—and eventually in producing it. But we must learn to walk before we can run.

One final comment should be made about beginning this journey. This last note is not so much a waypoint on the road as it is a caution about how we walk down it. For whatever reason, the immense learning that can happen in the early stages of studying theology often comes with an unfortunate side effect. There is a kind of pride that can emerge at the beginning of this journey, and it is as detrimental to healthy theology as it is common. This is particularly common during the first term of seminary studies. It is rooted, I suspect, in a genuine excitement in learning so many new and interesting things. But it often shows itself as an unappealing combination of arrogance and fervor to enlighten the unenlightened.

Two particular dangers are lurking when this happens. The first is that students who have had a class or two in church history or biblical studies begins to feel part of a very exclusive club—and they want to make sure that all of their friends and family know it. Perhaps understandably, it is tempting to show off one's new grasp of technical terminology or acquaintance with ancient writers. But in all the excitement, it can be difficult to see how off-putting this can be. We must be attentive to those occasions when we find a kind of secret delight in knowing something that others may not,

---

4. C. S. Lewis makes a very good case for this in his thought-provoking preface to Saint Athanasius's *On the Incarnation*.

particularly if those others have been a key part of our journey of faith. The moment we notice that our excitement is about *having* knowledge rather than about the *subject* of that knowledge, we can be sure something has gone wrong.

The second danger is that the new student will set out to correct all of the ignorance they now perceive in their fellow Christians. Again, there is something understandable about this. We have learned something eye-opening, and we want the eyes of others to be open as well. It's usually also true that family, friends, and church members will genuinely want to hear what a budding theology student is learning. But this can quickly turn to disaster if care is not taken. First-year seminary students who have had a week on Gnosticism or Arianism may take it upon themselves to root out any hint of these heresies in sermons they hear, in song lyrics they encounter, or even in casual conversations over coffee. The problem at this stage is that our emerging theologian does not yet have the grasp of the whole span of Christian doctrine to take on this role. Explanations that were so clear and enlightening in the introductory textbook or in a class lecture can get badly muddled in the translation. Bungled attempts to answer good and fair questions often lead to exasperation: "It made much more sense in class—I wish you just could have been there!"

The good news in all of this is that, with care, the time will come when those we love will benefit from what we are learning. But that may not happen in the ways we expect. We have to be patient, and even more important, we have to be humble. It is very important to remember that the heart of theological study is to learn to love God with our minds, and self-satisfied arrogance has no place in that learning process. When we begin to take in the sheer beauty of the Christian faith, the best next step is to go deeper. By keeping our focus on knowing and loving God in the midst of all we are learning, we will in fact be in a better position to help others see that beauty in the long run. This is a time to avoid any temptation to overestimate what we have already learned. And it is a time to feed the hunger to learn more and more, humbly and reverently, all toward the end of loving and worshiping God.

In the early stages of studying theology, as at every stage, it is important to remember that we are here because of testimony. We have encountered someone—a parent, a pastor, a friend—who has shared with us the good news that God has acted in the world in order to heal the world. In doing so, that someone was faithful to the charge that Jesus gave to the apostolic community to serve as his witnesses to the ends of the earth. And in time, our own journey of studying theology will help us to play an ongoing part in that story. As long as we keep our eyes fixed squarely on the God made known in Jesus—and not on our own accumulation of knowledge—we will be able to do that faithfully. The two disciples on the Emmaus road began by discussing the testimony they had heard about the empty tomb. On that road they found themselves in the company of the risen Jesus himself. Their posture of walking with Jesus along the road is a good picture of where the work of theology is intended to lead us. So to that part of the story we now turn.

Chapter 2: The Walk with Jesus

TOWARD THE END OF the Emmaus story, the two disciples reflect back on the walk they had just taken with the risen Jesus. "Were not our hearts burning within us," they say to each other, "while he was talking to us on the road, while he was opening the scriptures to us?" (v. 32). The statement seems to indicate both their astonishment at learning that their companion was Jesus himself and the delight they had felt in his company. The conversation along the road had helped them to understand the activity of God that had unfolded in the preceding days. They had assumed that Jesus's crucifixion meant that he could not be the one who would redeem Israel (v. 21). But as Jesus interpreted Israel's Scriptures to them while they walked, they came to realize that his suffering was part of the role of the messiah (v. 26).

This walk along the road points to a key insight about the nature of theology: *Christian theology is done in company with God.* Everything that we might know about God is drawn from God's self-revelation. There is nothing we can learn of God against his will. In this respect, theology is different from other areas of study. We typically do not think of the subjects of other disciplines—rock samples, works of literature, the monetary policy of a particular nation's government, etc.—as agents who choose to reveal themselves. We find something a bit closer in social sciences such as psychology or sociology, where research sometimes involves human beings who can choose to reveal themselves.

And of course professional ethics requires that research involving human subjects must obtain the consent of participants. But it remains the case that researchers often discover things about their subjects that those people did not intend to reveal (or even things they didn't know about themselves). Only in the case of theology are we directly dependent on the will of the subject of study for *anything* we might learn.

Furthermore, the kind of relationship that we cultivate with God shapes what we are able to know about him.[1] The disciples came to understand Jesus's role as messiah by walking with him and listening to him attentively. The focus of the conversation was still on the activity of God, as we explored in the last chapter. But they were able to make sense of those events only in the presence of the one who was at the center of that activity. This signals that God's self-revelation is not only aimed at increasing our knowledge. God could surely have done that through distant and impersonal means. Rather, God's self-revelation is aimed at cultivating a particular kind of relationship with us. And this suggests that the work of theology can only be done well in the context of that kind of relationship.

But what does this mean in practice? Cleopas and the other disciple had the advantage of the risen Jesus in the flesh walking on the road with them. For those of us on this side of Jesus's ascension to heaven, what does theology in the company of Jesus look like? The first mark of such theology must surely be prayer. And indeed, there is a deep connection in the Christian tradition between prayer and faithful theology. This was expressed with striking directness by the fourth-century monk Evagrius Ponticus: "If you are a theologian, you will pray truly, and if you pray truly, you will be a theologian."[2] Evagrius recognized that there is an understanding of God implicit in every prayer. As we express praise and gratitude toward God in

1. Paul K. Moser makes a very interesting case for this claim at a philosophical level in his book *The Elusive God*. Moser argues that knowledge of God is available to people purposively—that is, in ways that align with God's purposes in self-revelation. In that light, knowledge of God is intrinsically connected to a particular kind of relationship with God.

2. Evagrius Ponticus, "Chapters on Prayer" 61 (Casiday, 192).

prayer, and as we bring petitions before God, we are communicating who we believe God to be. But even more, this connection between theology and prayer makes clear the aim of studying theology. The whole point of knowing more *about* God is to *know God* more, to be drawn into communion with him. And prayer is one of the purest forms of that communion that we have.

I suspect that most people who are drawn to the study of theology have some form of active prayer life. But too often that prayer life is isolated from the reading, writing, and conversation that mark the day-to-day work of theology. This is a danger at any stage, but it is especially important to watch for this at the beginning of your theological journey. It can be disorienting to encounter new ideas and to learn things you've never known about Christianity. Students sometimes react to this feeling by distancing their studies from their prayer life, which feels familiar and reassuring in the midst of so much change. Add to that the fact that (at least in formal theology classes) there are grades, deadlines, and academic protocols to worry about. It is understandable to want to keep all of that separate from a relationship with God that is deeply personal. The thought of bringing them together can feel dangerous, as if what is most cherished in your life might now be up for debate.

Theology that is isolated from the life of prayer, however, misses its very purpose. If the study of theology is aimed at deepening communion with God, then prayer is a necessary practice. Continual prayer helps to form in us the very habits that enable us to know God more deeply: attentive listening, the articulation of our needs and desires before God, and most important, the submission of our wills to the divine will. These are the very marks of Jesus's own prayers in the New Testament, such as the Lord's Prayer (Matthew 6), the High Priestly Prayer (John 17), and his prayer in Gethsemane (Matthew 26 and parallel passages). Jesus's life continually revealed the eternal intimacy that God the Son shares with God the Father.[3] We see that in the prayers of Jesus.

---

3. This point is made with remarkable clarity by Pope Benedict XVI in *Jesus of Nazareth*, 1:6–7.

But we also see the incarnate Son aligning his human will to the divine will. When the Gospel narratives invite us to listen in on these prayers of the Son to the Father, we are thus given a model for our own prayers. In the very practice of submitting our wills to God in prayer, we are drawn into the eternal intimacy shared between the Father and the Son.

Does all of this mean that a student of theology should stop and pray before completing each assignment or attending each class? Frankly, I think this is a good practice to set at the beginning of one's journey in theology (and to continue throughout that journey). Even more, though, it means understanding the study of theology as *part* of one's prayer life. In each text we read, in each class session, in each assignment we write, we are aiming to deepen our love for God. We seek continually to walk in the company of God, to listen attentively, and to submit our own desires to the will of God. Obviously, this is not meant to suggest that our studies should replace the actual practice of prayer. Rather, we should understand both activities as drawing us toward the same goal: a deeper union with God. As you proceed, you will likely find that your learning will sharpen the focus of your prayer life and that continual prayer will keep your learning on its proper track.

It is thus crucial in the early days of studying theology to pay close attention to your prayer life. If you find yourself praying less— or not praying at all—make it a priority to devote plenty of time to this spiritual discipline. You might feel like you don't have time to pray, but that is something like saying that we don't have time to breathe because we're too busy trying to live. Prayer is the oxygen of healthy theology. You also might find yourself praying differently in these early days. This can be positive or negative, depending on how your prayers have changed. If you find renewed intensity and greater depth in your prayer life, then that is a very good sign indeed. But take caution if you discover that your prayers are becoming a kind of performance before God. When you are learning so much in your classes, there is a natural instinct to want to clean up the content of your prayers. Unfortunately, this can have the effect of distancing us from God and inhibiting the very communion with God that we are seeking in prayer.

A good practice in such times is to bring all that you are experiencing into your prayers. Bring your desire to pray in ways that are faithful to God's self-revelation. Bring the disorientation that you might be feeling from what you are learning. Bring even your sense of awkwardness in prayer if you feel self-conscious about what you are saying in your prayers. Bring all of these into the presence of God in prayer. It is precisely in openness before God that our souls can be aligned more and more to what God wills for us. The Psalms provide a useful model of this kind of raw openness in God's presence. We see in those prayers the full range of human experience and emotion, reminding us that we can draw near to God as we are.[4] The Psalms call us to carry our questions before God in prayer rather than trying to live with our minds divided from our souls. Theology in the company of God is part of a life of prayer.

A second mark of theology in God's presence is attentiveness to God. The disciples listened with their hearts burning as Jesus unfolded the Scriptures to them. But in the present, where might we focus our attention to do the same as we study theology? The first and most central answer to that question is the Bible. The canon of Scripture has long been recognized as God's word to God's people, and so it is natural to read it attentively if we wish to hear from God. As any first-year theology student comes to learn, of course, the interpretation of the Bible can be a complicated matter. But *that* theology must attend carefully to the biblical text is not in doubt. Just as Scripture was at the center of Jesus's conversation with the disciples on the Emmaus road, so also is it at the heart of faithful theology. We will explore this in greater detail in chapter 3.

Attentiveness to God can also be focused on other texts that we read in our exploration of theology. It must be said immediately that these other texts, even the classics, are not canonical Scripture. They should not be treated as if they hold the same level

4. April Yamasaki provides a helpful set of reflections on the Psalms as a model of prayer in her chapter "Praying It Like It Is" in *Sacred Pauses,* 55–64.

of authority as biblical texts. But classic texts are important bearers of the Christian tradition over time and space. These works have stood the test of time because they witness faithfully to God's saving activity. Readings that have pointed generations of Christians toward God's self-revelation are worthy of our careful attention. This can also be true of contemporary books. But because those are more recent and have not undergone the sifting process that happens over time, a level of caution is appropriate. God can speak through a new book as well as an old book, but we should certainly not suppose that a book reflects the voice of God simply because it is a published work of theology. As we listen carefully to classic and contemporary voices, we should always ask if those voices are pointing faithfully to the God revealed in Jesus.

And this leads us naturally to our teachers. It is difficult to imagine any person, even one who reads a lot of books, making much progress in theology without good teachers. So attentiveness to God can also be expressed through listening carefully to those who introduce us to the riches of the Christian tradition. But here, as with the things that we read, we must be very careful. Scripture has plenty to say about teachers who mislead their students, and those texts are sobering indeed.[5] If we take it as obvious that not everything a theology professor says reflects the voice of God, then we have to ask how we might listen thoughtfully. Here it is important to look both to the content of what is taught and to the character of the teacher. Does the content focus on God's character and activity? Is it centered in the Scriptures, as read by the community of faith over time and space? Does the teacher model a love for God and a desire to cultivate a deeper relationship with God? There is no question that God can still speak through an imperfect teacher. But respecting the knowledge and credentials of our teachers is not the same thing as trusting them to guide our souls closer to God. The latter should come only with considerable time and experience, as we prayerfully listen for God's voice in the midst of our classes and studies.

---

5. Jas 3:1 and 2 Pet 2:1–3 are just two examples.

So prayer and attentiveness are two marks of theology in the company of God. A third can be found in the posture that we rightly take before the living God. There is a vast difference between the Creator and creatures such as ourselves, and awareness of that difference leads to a proper reverence before God. And it is perhaps this third mark that is most evidently lacking in (at least some) academic theology nowadays. We live in a society that rewards swagger and playful irreverence, and unfortunately that attitude is sometimes reflected even among professional theologians. But reverence before God is appropriate for theology at any stage, from the beginner to the seasoned veteran. In writing, speaking, and other public expressions of theology, a flippant tone is a sure sign that something has gone wrong. Such public performances may be aimed at self-promotion or cultivating a broader audience, but they are not directed toward theology in the company of God.

Why is cultivating and maintaining reverence a challenge as we progress in the study of theology? Without question, an element of the arrogance that we explored in chapter 1 is often involved. As we begin to sense that we now know what the average layperson may not, we can begin to communicate in a tone that is mocking or derisive toward the perceived ignorance around us (which we may have shared a few short months ago!). I also suspect that the feeling of breaking boundaries or shattering taboos is exhilarating to many people. A posture of humble reverence may seem to such folks, consciously or unconsciously, to be at odds with truly groundbreaking theological insights. I fully recognize that this sort of irreverence is not always directed toward God. My sense is that a flippant tone is most often aimed at those who have been perceived to misuse power in the church. But still such a tone is telling. Playful irreverence in theology suggests that one is primarily conscious of human audiences, including both the people one is attacking and those who are likely to applaud such attacks. But it does not suggest a sense that theology is being done *in God's presence.* To read, write, and discuss theology in God's company means that we are first and foremost conscious of the divine presence. The tone and content of our words should thus be fitting to that primary reality.

In fairness, it is natural to ask if the disciples on the Emmaus road demonstrate the kind of reverence we have in mind here. We must admit that there is a sharpness in the question that Cleopas asked Jesus in Luke 24:18: "Are you the only stranger in Jerusalem who does not know the things that have taken place there in these days?" But that edge clearly comes from the seriousness with which Cleopas takes these matters. More important, the disciples at this stage do not realize with whom they are dealing. The question comes at the beginning of the conversation, before Jesus scolds them in verses 25–26. From that point on, Jesus does most of the talking as the disciples listen with burning hearts. While it is implicit in the text rather than explicit, we can detect a quiet reverence in the disciples the more they listen to Jesus. It sets in gradually in the movement from Cleopas's searing question to their posture of listening. This posture is fitting for people in the presence of the incarnate Son, and these disciples intuitively (if gradually) take that posture even before they know his identity.

A fourth mark of theology in the company of God goes hand-in-hand with reverence, even if it seems at first to cut in the other direction. To be in the presence of God is to reflect the deep joy of souls that have found their home. This joy will manifest itself in the process of knowing and loving God more deeply, which is the very aim of studying theology. The experience we have in mind here is quite different from the lighthearted irreverence we explored above, which often is fueled by a kind of underlying bitterness. Proper joy is fully compatible with, and in fact depends on, reverence at being in the company of God. This is precisely why the quiet reverence of the walk on the Emmaus road gives way to the exuberant outburst of verse 32: "Were not our hearts burning within us while he was talking to us on the road, while he was opening the scriptures to us?"

It is important to clarify that this characteristic of theology in God's presence is a bit different from the three we have explored so far. For prayerfulness, attentiveness, and reverence are qualities that we must strive to cultivate. By contrast, joy is not something that we muster through effort; rather, it is an outflow of being in the presence of God. In this respect it is not as directly under our control as the other three marks. But joy is still an important signal of how we are going about our studies. If we find that joy is continually missing from our learning, then perhaps that is an indication that we are trying to go about our work in a way that is isolated from our relationship with God. This can bring a heaviness in the soul that seems to grow the deeper you go. In such times the focus of theology might be about God, but it is likely not being done in the presence of God. If you notice these dynamics in the course of your own studies, it is wise to pay attention.

A word of reasonable caution is in order here. This does not mean that theology in the company of God will be free of challenges. A difficult class or a frustrating text is to be expected from time to time. And often the process of growth and learning involves a kind of temporary disorientation. There will be days when you find yourself confused or unsure of yourself, and there will be days when you are struggling to keep up with all that needs to be done. All of this is part of the journey. If you are trying to walk that road in the company of God, however, it won't take long to get glimpses of a deep and abiding joy. A persistent dread is an indicator that some wrong approach has been taken. And more often than not, the problem is that the student has tried to walk the path of knowledge without the fellowship of the one who is the way, the truth, and the life (John 14:6).

So the Emmaus road teaches us that theology is meant to be bathed in prayer, pursued with attentiveness, marked by reverence, and seasoned with joy. Yet it also hints at one other reality. The disciples were in the company of Jesus before they realized it; their awareness of his presence along the road came mainly in retrospect. Something similar happens for many of us when we begin to explore the Christian tradition in depth. Even in the midst of so much that is new and even strange, we get a glimpse of something that feels familiar. We now see a fuller revelation of a God who has been present and active throughout our lives, whether or not we recognized it at the time. The study of Christianity jogs memories of pointers to God's presence in our prior lives that we perhaps felt more than understood.

In reflecting on his own surprising conversion to Christian faith, author Frederick Buechner describes a similar experience:

> Though I was brought up in a family where church played virtually no role at all, through a series of events from childhood on I was moved, for the most part without any inkling of it, closer and closer to a feeling for that Mystery out of which the church arose in the first place until, finally, the Mystery itself came to have a face for me, and the face it came to have for me was the face of Christ. It was a slow, obscure process . . .[6]

What Buechner describes is a kind of Emmaus encounter. He was drawn to this mysterious other until the recognition set in that the other was Jesus himself. That recognition enabled him to see in retrospect many significant moments of God's presence in his life, which he narrates in *Now and Then* and its predecessor, *The Sacred Journey*.[7]

It is worth identifying two significant features of these moments in which we recognize God's prior presence in our lives. First, we should understand that the agent who draws us toward Christ is the Holy Spirit, the third person of the Trinity. Granted, the Spirit's role is not made particularly explicit in the Emmaus narrative (or in the Buechner memoir, for that matter). But the Christian tradition has long recognized that a distinct work of the Spirit is to draw us toward Christ, even in seasons of our lives when we may not be expecting or seeking that.[8] And this is precisely what we see when the disciples recognized that their hearts were burning in the yet-unknown presence of Jesus. Similarly, note that Buechner uses the passive voice above to recall that he

---

6. Buechner, *Now and Then*, 4–5.

7. Buechner, *Sacred Journey*.

8. Two of the many New Testament texts that address this work of the Holy Spirit are 1 Cor 2 and John 16. I also explore this work of the Spirit in *Radiance of God*, 66–81.

"was moved" closer and closer to a feeling for the mystery that he came to recognize as Christ. While Buechner is somewhat coy in that passage about identifying the one who moved him, this is distinctly the activity of the Holy Spirit. In those moments in our own lives when we look back and see the presence of Christ, it is the Spirit who enables us to recognize it.

The second feature is that these encounters with Christ are movements from relative obscurity toward greater clarity. The disciples' experience at Emmaus came together for them when they recognized that their companion was Jesus. They made their way quickly to Jerusalem to share the news with the other disciples because they finally understood the significance of God's activity in Jesus, including their own experience along the road. They realized the importance of their conversation with Jesus when they recognized him, and not before. So it would be a considerable mistake to read the Emmaus story as a generic affirmation of experience itself as revealing God's nature and purposes—even if we rightly recognize that God is present in that experience. The disciples' experience along the road was pointing them toward a specific understanding of God's action in the death and resurrection of Jesus. They simply would not have fathomed what God had done if they had not come to see who their mysterious companion actually was. In the same way, our own experiences of God's unrecognized presence become revelatory only in explicit connection to Jesus and the community of his disciples. Indeed, the very purpose of those divine movements is to draw us toward a clearer vision—and therefore a deeper love—of the God who accompanies us.

This second point will be important to keep in mind throughout your journey in the study of theology. Too often, two distinct claims get confused. It is good and necessary to affirm that God is at work, particularly in the person of the Holy Spirit, broadly and widely in our experiences to draw us toward Christ. And as we've been exploring, this can happen before we recognize that God is at work in this way. But this is often taken to mean something very different; namely, that the presence of God in our prior experience was all that we needed. The point of the Emmaus narrative is not that the disciples' journey was complete along the road. It is true that they were in the presence of Jesus, but they needed to get to Emmaus. They needed Jesus to be made known to them in the breaking of the bread. The walk with Jesus and their burning hearts were leading them somewhere, and it was at that sacred meal that they understood what God had been doing.

The point here is that God has been present in your life, leading you to this time and place. Your study of theology is a means of coming to greater knowledge and love of the one who has been with you all along. It will not always be a straight line from obscurity to greater clarity, as there will be times of disorientation and confusion. But the reason you're here is to see more clearly what God has been doing. And this happens when we undertake theology in the company of that same God. In those moments when we encounter a familiar echo in the study of Scripture or church history or doctrine, we should take it as a good sign. Those glimpses of recognition indicate that the God who has accompanied us along our road is the same God who has accompanied the saints of all times and places. The men and women of the past (and present) that we meet in our studies are pointing to a God who desires to be known and therefore has made himself known in Jesus. And they are pointing us toward the same destination where the Spirit has been leading us all along the way. The work of theology is, therefore, taking us to Emmaus, a place of fellowship, recognition, and joy.

One last observation is in order. The two disciples in this story come to a moment of clarity at Emmaus about all that God had been doing in Jesus. But that moment of clarity is not by any means the end of their story. In many ways, it is just the beginning. They immediately get up and set out for Jerusalem to connect with the other disciples, as we will explore in chapter 7. And the resurrection appearances of Jesus that we find at the end of Luke's Gospel, including Emmaus, will serve as the basis of the church's testimony in Luke's book of Acts. In the power of the Spirit, who comes upon them in Acts 2, the community of disciples will continue to walk in the presence of God as they engage in ministry. The story of Acts is largely the story of the church growing deeper in fellowship with God even as they invite the world into that fellowship through testimony to the resurrection of Jesus.

All of this is good news for those of us studying theology. Just as with the disciples, our Emmaus moments of recognition are not the end of our stories. This is true in the sense that the work of theology continues long beyond our formal studies in support of our various ministries in the life of the church. It is good and necessary to continue reading, writing, and engaging in conversation with the community of faith as we also testify to the resurrection in words and actions. But this point is also true in the sense that theology is aimed at deepening our communion with God, and that is a communion that never ends. In our walks with Jesus, recognized and unrecognized, we are cultivating a relationship that is at the center of our purpose, both in this life and in eternity.

In each book that you read, in each class that you attend, and in each assignment that you prepare, then, I encourage you to seek the companionship of Jesus. Thanks to the ongoing work of the Holy Spirit, our eyes can be opened to the presence of Jesus along the roads that we walk. And as we seek to remain in his company, we will find that those roads lead us to deeper communion with God—just as it did for the disciples of Luke 24. They found their hearts burning as Jesus opened the Scriptures to them. In the same way, the Bible is at the center of our walk with Jesus. So in chapter 3 we will explore the work of theology as an immersion in Scripture.

Chapter 3: The Opening of the Scriptures

IN ACTS 8:26–40, WE find a story about reading Scripture while traveling along a road. An Ethiopian court official had come to Jerusalem to worship Israel's God, and on the way home he was reading the prophet Isaiah. The Holy Spirit prompted Philip, one of the members of the early Christian community, to go and join the court official's chariot. He asked if the official understood what he was reading, and the reply was direct and honest: "How can I, unless someone guides me?" Philip accepted the official's invitation to sit beside him in the chariot, and the pressing question was whom the text was about (in this case, Isa 53). In response, Philip "proclaimed to him the good news about Jesus." This conversation along the road about Israel's Scripture led to the proclamation of the gospel and ultimately to the court official's baptism.

There are a number of interesting echoes of the Emmaus story in this passage (and both stories, we will recall, come to us from the same author). Both conversations take place during a journey on a road. Both involve a mysterious stranger interpreting those ancient texts in light of Jesus. Both signal a central Christian sacrament (communion in the first; baptism in the second). And both end with the disappearance of the mysterious stranger. Above all, these texts point to a central reality of the study of theology: *Christian theology is grounded in the canonical Scriptures.* Just as the conversation between Philip and the Ethiopian court official centered on a biblical text, so also did Jesus's discussion with the disciples on the Emmaus road focus on Scripture: "Beginning with Moses and all the prophets, he interpreted to them the things about himself in all the Scriptures" (Luke 24:27). In this chapter, we explore the essential place of the Bible in Christian theology.

We begin with a very basic question: Why? Why does theology need always to remain attentive to the Bible? When theological reflection has become disconnected from the Scriptures, why should we conclude that it has lost its way? The first and most direct response to this question is that the Bible witnesses to divine revelation. Recall our central point from chapter 1 that theology begins with testimony to the saving activity of God. Scripture is the sacred witness to those divine actions. So theology cannot even properly get off the ground without attention to the Bible. It is true that the good news of Jesus's life, death, and resurrection is often proclaimed with words that we speak—but that proclamation must always be grounded in the biblical witness. And as questions arise in the life of faith that require theological reflection, we depend on God's self-revelation to address those questions. Because the canonical Scriptures point us toward that divine self-disclosure, they are the lifeblood of Christian theology.

It is worth observing that the disciples walking the Emmaus road with Jesus were discussing the only Scriptures available to them at the time: Israel's Scriptures, which Christians now call the Old Testament. And this is an important signal to us about the place of the Old Testament in the Christian biblical canon. While the saving actions of God are centered in the life, death, and resurrection of Jesus, the biblical story begins long before those events. The Old Testament is the story of the people of Israel, and it is essential for understanding what God was doing in and through Jesus. This point becomes very clear when we make a second and rather startling observation about the Emmaus text. At the most basic and obvious level, Jesus does not show up in the Bible until the New Testament. And yet recall that verse 27 of Luke 24 tells us that Jesus "interpreted to them the things about himself in all the Scriptures." The phrase "about himself" is enough to stop us

MADE KNOWN TO THEM

in our tracks—if Jesus doesn't show up until the New Testament, how is the Old Testament about him?

Two words will help us to see how this is the case: expectation and vocation. The narrative of the Old Testament leaves the reader with a clear sense that God's redemptive work is not yet finished. Something is yet to happen, and the note of expectation and longing provides an important context for understanding Jesus's entry onto the scene. As Tom Wright suggests, "Israel's ancient Scriptures are framed with a narrative, an unfinished narrative of a certain shape and type." The reader is left "with a sense that this story is supposed to be going somewhere, but that it hasn't got there yet. It is an unfinished narrative, an unfinished *agenda*. Things are supposed to happen that haven't happened yet."[1] This is precisely the story into which Jesus steps, as a member of faithful Israel. The New Testament texts as a whole, and the Gospels in particular, understand Jesus as the fulfillment of this expectation. It is the activity of Jesus that completes the narrative. This is why the New Testament authors take such great pains to show the actions of Jesus as representing the fulfillment of God's promises as attested throughout Israel's Scriptures. And for all of the diversity in the biblical witnesses to Jesus's life and deeds, there is significant unity among them in seeing Jesus in precisely this way. Wright contends that "unless we are constantly aware, in reading the Gospels, that they are telling the Jesus story in such a way as to bring out the Israel story, we will never hear their proper harmony."[2] We certainly see this in the Emmaus narrative. The suffering and eventual glory of the messiah, declared by the prophets, is identified directly with what has happened to Jesus (vv. 25–26). Israel's story has come to its climax.

The word vocation is also important in helping us understand how the Old Testament could point to Jesus. For here we see

1. Wright, *How God Became King*, 50–51 (original emphasis).

2. Wright, *How God Became King*, 59. Wright makes the important additional point that the life, death, and resurrection of Jesus was not the way that Israel was expecting those divine promises to be fulfilled. This contrast between the actual fulfillment and the expected manner of fulfillment sets up a significant point of tension in the New Testament.

precisely what was at the heart of Israel's story. It was a particular vocation; specifically, a calling to bless the nations. We see this in the calling of Abram (later Abraham) in Genesis 12. After calling Abram to go to the land that will be shown to him, the Lord promises to make him into a great nation (v. 2). And the conclusion of that foundational call story shows that this nation was always meant to serve the entire world: "And all peoples on earth will be blessed through you" (v. 3). Israel is reminded of this vocation in various ways throughout the Old Testament, most notably in the book of Isaiah. One helpful example for our purposes is Isaiah 49, which describes a servant who apparently is to be understood as the people of Israel (v. 3). The calling of this servant is expressed in 49:6: "I will give you as a light to the nations, that my salvation may reach to the end of the earth." This is an echo, then, of the very purpose for which God had brought Abram's descendants together as a nation. And Isaiah's use of light to describe this blessing of the nations (we see it also in Isa 42 and 60) is of particular interest to the author of Luke and Acts.

From the beginning of the Gospel of Luke, it is clear that Jesus is to be understood as the one who takes up Israel's calling as a light to the nations. One story where this comes through beautifully is in the presentation of the infant Jesus in the temple in Luke 2:22–38. There we read about a righteous and devout man named Simeon who was "looking forward to the consolation of Israel." The Holy Spirit had revealed to him that he would not die before he saw the Lord's messiah. Now that same Spirit had led Simeon into the temple where Jesus was being presented by his parents. He took Jesus in his arms and offered a memorable prayer, knowing that the promise had been fulfilled:

> Master, now you are dismissing your servant in peace,
> according to your word,
> for my eyes have seen your salvation,
> which you have prepared in the presence of all peoples,
> a light for revelation to the gentiles
> and for glory to your people Israel.

Not only did Simeon recognize this child as the promised messiah, but he also saw that Jesus would fulfill Israel's calling as a light to all the nations.

If the life, death, and resurrection of Jesus represent the divine actions that bring salvation to the nations, then the proclamation of those events by Jesus's disciples are a crucial part of Israel's story. And that Spirit-empowered proclamation is just what we see in Acts. On two occasions, the image of light to the nations (so important in Isaiah) gets used to express the impact of Jesus's saving work. The first is in Acts 13, where Paul and Barnabas are speaking to the crowds gathered at the synagogue in Antioch of Pisidia. When their message is resisted by the people who are listening, they appeal to the Isa 49:6 passage that we explored above. Paul and Barnabas highlight the Lord's command to be a light to the gentiles and bring salvation to the ends of the earth. (We should note that this also recalls Jesus's own words to the apostles in Acts 1:8 that they would be his witnesses "to the ends of the earth.") When the gentiles hear this, they respond with gladness and praise (13:48).

Later in Acts, in chapter 26, Paul gives his defense before King Agrippa. After narrating his dramatic conversion and call story, he describes his evangelistic ministry. For our purposes, verses 22–23 are particularly interesting: "To this day I have had help from God, and so I stand here, testifying to both small and great, saying nothing but what the prophets and Moses said would take place: that the messiah must suffer and that, by being the first to rise from the dead, he would proclaim light both to our people and to the gentiles." The first thing to notice is Paul's claim that Moses and the prophets had prophesied that the messiah must suffer, just as Jesus had told the disciples on the Emmaus road in Luke. Again, then, the pivotal events of Jesus's story are seen as the fulfillment of Old Testament expectation. Like Jesus, Paul asserts that the messiah's suffering should not come as a surprise to anyone rightly reading Israel's sacred texts. The second thing to notice is that Paul understands Jesus's resurrection as the key to proclaiming the light to the gentiles as well as to the people of Israel. The message is rather clear in the narrative we find in Luke and Acts. Israel's calling, given to Abram and affirmed by Isaiah, was to bless the nations as a light that brings salvation. Now Jesus has taken up and fulfilled that calling in his death and resurrection, as foreseen by Simeon and announced broadly by Paul. The many gentiles in Acts who respond to the gospel and become believers are the fruit of God's intention from the beginning. Jesus's story is Israel's story.

The work of Christian theology is a response to this story of what God has done. God has revealed himself in the activity that heals the world, and theology is sustained reflection on that self-disclosure. The Christian Scriptures, both the Old and the New Testaments, bear witness to this divine self-revelation. Not only do they narrate the events by which God has revealed himself, but they also offer Spirit-guided interpretation of the significance of those events. For that reason, the Bible must always be at the center of theological reflection. Just as Jesus's discussion with the disciples on the Emmaus road involved an opening of the Scriptures, so also the ongoing work of theology must pay careful attention to "the things about [Jesus] in all the Scriptures" (Luke 24:27). What we say (and sing) about God in the various modes of theology—books, articles, hymns, sermons, lectures, conversations, etc.—emerges from our Spirit-illumined reflection on the biblical text.

And if we recall from chapter 2 that the ultimate aim of theology is to draw us into deeper communion with God, then we are led to a second reason why the Bible must be part of that work: reading Scripture shapes us in Christ-likeness. The Holy Spirit draws us deeper into the life and love of the Triune God in a variety of ways. And central among them is prayerful immersion in the text of Scripture. Reading the Bible is a formative task in the Christian life, and this is certainly true when it comes to the work of theology. As we come to know more *about* God by attending to the biblical witness, we ultimately strive to *know and serve* God more deeply and faithfully. The Spirit's work in shaping us in the likeness of Christ will then bear fruit in evident ways in our lives. The role of Scripture in this process is at the heart of Paul's comment at the conclusion of 2 Tim 3. After encouraging Timothy to continue in what he has learned and firmly believed, he offers a reminder: "From childhood you have known sacred writings that are able to instruct you for salvation through faith in Christ Jesus" (3:15). Paul then turns from the cognitive emphasis on instruction to a broader understanding of formation through reading the Bible: "All Scripture is inspired by God and is useful for teaching, for reproof, for correction, and for training in righteousness, so that the person of God may be proficient, equipped for every good work" (3:16–17). The reverence expressed here for the biblical text is matched by the high regard for its practical usefulness in the life of faith, including the task of theology.

It is important to be clear about what is at stake. Scripture gives us access to knowledge of the saving work of God in the story of Israel, centered in the life, death, and resurrection of Jesus. But it also forms us, by the Holy Spirit's agency, as people who are shaped by that saving work of God. That is to say that the Bible does not just provide us with information; in the Spirit's hands, it makes us into new people. It is true that theology has a natural connection to the cognitive dimension of this transformation. Knowledge of God is important, and the change that God aims to accomplish within us involves a renewal of the mind (Rom 12:2). But the Holy Spirit's sanctifying work reshapes the entire person according to the likeness of Christ. At its best, Christian theology does not just talk about this transformation—it immerses us in the Spirit's sanctifying work. In that light, the Bible is not merely a record of what God does. The Bible is a means of encountering the Spirit that draws our entire lives into that saving activity.

So as a sacred witness to divine revelation and as a means of the Holy Spirit's sanctifying work, Scripture is at the heart of the work of theology. Yet if we consider what it is that draws us toward this transformative story, we find a third reason for the Bible's importance. Scripture reflects the radiant beauty of God and thereby captivates our hearts. In that light, what keeps us moving forward in the journey of Christian theology is the desire to be in the company of the God we encounter in the pages of the Bible. The disciples at Emmaus captured this experience as they reflected on their time with the risen Jesus: "Were not our hearts burning within us while he was talking to us on the road, while he was opening the Scriptures to us?" (Luke 24:32). We can reasonably presume that this desire is a major part of why the disciples pleaded with Jesus to remain with them at Emmaus, as we will explore in the next chapter. To encounter the beauty of God in the biblical story is to long to remain in the company of that God. As many theology students find in their first Bible classes, getting a taste of Scripture makes us hungry for more. And at the core of that longing is a desire for the God revealed in its pages.

We get a beautiful glimpse of this in the opening lines of the Psalter in the Old Testament. The first Psalm begins with a contrast between two ways of living:

> Happy are those
> who do not follow the advice of the wicked
> or take the path that sinners tread
>   or sit in the seat of scoffers,
> but their delight is in the law of the Lord,
>   and on his law they meditate day and night.
> They are like trees
>   planted by streams of water,
> which yield their fruit in its season,
>   and their leaves do not wither.
> In all that they do, they prosper. (Ps 1:1–3)

While there is a clear sense in these lines that there is a practical value in taking guidance from the law of the Lord, that practical value is not the primary motivator. The word "delight" is the key. Those who meditate on God's law do so because they long to do so, to be in the company of the God who gave it. The resulting stability and fruitfulness emerge because the one who delights in the law of the Lord has recognized God as the highest good. While theologians rightly pursue truth, therefore, that truth is always connected with goodness and beauty. And the actual pursuit of these necessarily engages the Scriptures in which the God who is truth, beauty, and goodness is made known.

So far in this chapter we have been exploring why the Bible must be at the center of theological study. We have seen that Scripture witnesses to divine revelation, forms us by the activity of the Holy Spirit in the likeness of Christ, and draws us toward the beauty and goodness of God. Now we turn to a related question: How should we read Scripture as we go about the work of theology? Our main concern here is not with the technical skills of biblical interpretation, which are developed over time under the guidance of experienced teachers. Rather, what we're after in this chapter is our posture and approach to Scripture as we go about the work of theology. What should our reading look like as we seek to know God more deeply through the Bible?

The question is posed with particular sharpness in the Emmaus passage. The conversation between Jesus and the disciples along the road makes it clear that Scripture is not self-interpreting.[3] Jesus's reprimand of these disciples in verses 25–26 was not because they did not know the Scriptures. Instead, the problem was that they knew them but could not see their meaning: that the messiah must suffer the things that Jesus had suffered before entering into his glory. The heart of the theological conversation that followed as they walked toward Emmaus was Jesus interpreting the Scriptures to them—Scriptures that they had long known. The disciples' recollection later that their hearts had been burning during this conversation includes a striking phrase: "while he was opening the Scriptures to us" (v. 32). As you embark on your formal theological training, this is a phrase worth keeping in mind. Without doubt, the text of Scripture is to be known and savored. But it is also to be "opened," as these disciples learned along the road. What posture can we take, then, that might help the Scriptures to be opened to us as we go about our work?

One important answer to this question is that we read the Bible with the apostolic community of faith. That is, the same church that has passed down these texts through the generations has also

---

3. See Koskela, "Authority of Scripture," 210–11.

reflected thoughtfully and prayerfully upon them. Those reflections are captured in many forms: creeds, confessions, sermons, liturgy, hymns, commentaries, and many other treasures that are part of the church's canonical heritage. These materials reflect the prayerful conversation about Scripture among God's people across two millennia. It would be unwise in the extreme to delve into biblical interpretation without paying attention to what has been said in that conversation thus far. The story from Acts 8 that we explored at the beginning of this chapter captures this point very clearly. When Philip asks the Ethiopian court official if he understands the biblical text that he is reading, the response is telling: "How can I, unless someone guides me?" (Acts 8:31). His invitation to Philip to join him in the chariot leads to a conversation about the meaning of the text from Isaiah. The court official recognizes the need to read Scripture with the guidance of the apostolic community in order to understand its significance.[4]

We might also note that the Holy Spirit guided Philip to go to the place where the court official's chariot was traveling (8:26) and to approach the chariot (8:29). This is an important cue for us about the role of the Holy Spirit in our practice of reading Scripture together. The apostolic community is a means that the Holy Spirit uses to open the Scriptures to us. It is true and important that the Spirit inspired the Bible, but we also recognize that the Spirit continues to illuminate and guide our reading of the Bible. And as the Acts 8 text reminds us, that reading is a specific kind of communal act. It is not just any group of people who open the Scriptures to us; it is the apostolic community of faith that was called by Jesus and empowered by the Holy Spirit. We need to be precise here, as the canonical Scriptures do hold an authority that other treasures of the church's heritage do not. But we can and should receive these other materials as gifts of the Spirit that immerse us in two millennia of reading Scripture thoughtfully and prayerfully. Across

4. The phrase "apostolic community" here signals a particular community that is rooted in the apostles' testimony to Jesus but includes many other ministers and evangelists. This is significant in the Acts 8 text in particular, since it is likely that this Philip is not the apostle Philip but rather the deacon named in Acts 6:5 (later called "Philip the evangelist" in Acts 21:8).

time and space, these writings, hymns, and liturgies can offer us the kind of guidance that Philip offered the court official in his chariot. And in each case, it is the Holy Spirit that draws believers together around the pages of sacred Scripture.

Recognizing the Spirit's role in our reading of the Bible leads us to a second point. Not only do we read together with the apostolic community, but we also read devotionally. That is, we read Scripture as a means of drawing into the presence of God. We read with an openness to hearing God's voice speaking through the Scriptures. In their early days of studying theology, many students struggle with the feeling that their devotional reading of the Bible is disconnected from their academic reading of the Bible. I would never discourage maintaining a consistent discipline of reading Scripture devotionally during your formal theological training; on the contrary, I would lift it up as an essential practice. Yet I would encourage students to bring those devotional sensibilities into their academic reading. I understand that some teachers may discourage this, implicitly or even explicitly. But typically the concern in those cases is that students will resist more technical tools of interpretation that can be very helpful in understanding a particular book or passage. That is not at all what I mean by devotional reading. It is a good thing for students to learn the various linguistic, historical, and literary tools that help our reading of the Bible. We can use these tools and still read with an openness to God's voice and presence being mediated through the text of Scripture. This is particularly important when we are reading Scripture theologically; that is, as a means for drawing us more deeply into knowledge of and communion with God. The work of theology fulfills its purpose when it is a means of encountering the living God, so it follows that we should approach Scripture in expectation of such an encounter.

One person who understood this well was the third-century theologian Origen. In book 4 of his treatise *On First Principles*, Origen offered an account of the inspiration of Scripture. He first outlined a number of prophecies from the Old Testament that anticipated the work of Christ. The fulfillment of these in the work of Jesus, he suggested, should be ample evidence of their truth and divine inspiration. He then turned to a second argument, one that emerges from the experience of reading the Bible itself. If approached properly, he suggested, Scripture mediates an encounter with God. "If anyone consider the prophetic sayings with all the diligence and reverence they deserve, it is certain that, in the very act, while he reads and carefully scrutinizes, his mind and senses having been touched by a divine breath, he will recognize what he reads to be not human utterances but the words of God."[5] Origen's main aim in this section is to emphasize the divine source of the Scriptures. But his phrasing perfectly captures the experience of being drawn into God's presence as we read. To feel our minds and our senses "touched by a divine breath" as we ponder the Bible is a sign that our studying is on course. If the work of theology is to draw us nearer to God with our minds and our hearts, then this is the approach to Scripture that is fitting to the task.

Origen's comment that the Scriptures deserve zeal and reverence leads us to a third point, one that follows naturally from the second. If reading the Bible is a means of encountering God, then we must approach it with reverence. This is really a corollary of the reverence for God that we explored in chapter 2. The study of theology is not only about becoming informed; it is about being formed by the Holy Spirit in the likeness of Christ. This formation necessarily involves a kind of change in us, as indicated by the Rom 12:2 text noted earlier in this chapter. The phrasing of that passage signals that we do not create this change in ourselves: "Be transformed by the renewing of the mind." Such a transformation requires trust in the God who is at work within us. We must be open to the various ways in which the Spirit might work to shape us—and this includes the Spirit's use of Scripture. Reverent reading, therefore, does not mean the worship of the text of Scripture; it means a sober openness to God's transformative work through our reading of Scripture.

But too often the Bible is approached very differently in theological conversations. When the importance of reverence is

---

5. Origen, *On First Principles* 4.1.6 (Behr, 475–77).

forgotten or dismissed, the Bible can be forced into a role it was never meant to play. Particular passages can be isolated and used as support for positions that have already been taken. Readers can arrogantly seek control over the text to advance a theological agenda already in place. We can be sure something has gone wrong when we are approaching Scripture to advance our own purposes rather than to be guided and shaped by God. By contrast, when we take a posture of humility and openness in reading the Bible, we recognize that it is a means by which God draws us ever more toward his purposes for us.

In the Ignatian tradition of spiritual discernment, there is a concept that provides a worthwhile analogy here. This idea can help us see what a reverent reading of Scripture involves. This concept is called indifference, and in the context of discernment, it is not at all what it sounds like. We often think of indifference as a lack of care or concern. But in spiritual discernment, indifference means a genuine openness to whatever guidance God might give. That is, we cannot enter into a process of true discernment if we are already attached to one particular outcome. It is only authentically discernment if we are honestly open to wherever God might lead us. This posture of openness is necessary if we are to place God's good will above any of our specific desires or plans. And there is something very similar at work in a reverent reading of Scripture. Just as we should not use the language of discernment simply to add divine approval to whatever plans we have already made, we should also avoid turning to Scripture simply to bolster whatever theological positions we already hold. As we meditate on the Bible in the course of our theological work, our aim should be to allow God to open the Scriptures to us.

Like the disciples along the Emmaus road, then, we walk with reverent attention to what God might reveal to us in and through his word. By prayerfully engaging the biblical text in the company of the apostolic community, we open ourselves to God's transformative work within and among us. This really is what is at the heart of theology. And as we do so, we will find that we are addressing the deepest hunger within us: the hunger for communion with

God. In fact, the transformative work of the Holy Spirit within us is aimed at drawing us deeper into this communion. And because we long for that communion above all else, getting a taste for theology makes us want more. This is exactly why the disciples plead with Jesus to stay once they arrive at the town of Emmaus. That part of the story is the focus of our next chapter.

Chapter 4: The Appeal to Remain

AT THE BEGINNING OF his book *For the Life of the World*, Orthodox theologian Alexander Schmemann makes the following observation: "In the biblical story of creation man is presented, first of all, as a hungry being, and the whole world as his food."[1] He describes the portrait of a banquet as "the central image of life" throughout the entire Bible. A bit later in the chapter, he takes up the question of the true object of our hunger. What, ultimately, are we seeking as we sit down to the great banquet table of the world? His answer: "The world as man's food is not something 'material' and limited to material functions, thus different from, and opposed to, the specifically 'spiritual' functions by which man is related to God. All that exists is God's gift to man, and it all exists to make God known to man, to make man's life communion with God."[2] The good gifts of creation are means of relating to the God who created us. And our physical hunger is a manifestation of a deeper hunger within, a longing that signals our very purpose as human beings. "Man is a hungry being. But he is hungry for God," Schmemann concludes. "Behind all the hunger of our life is God. All desire is finally a desire for him."[3]

The Emmaus story is a story about a journey, but it is also a story about eating. The central event in the story once they reach

1. Schmemann, *For the Life of the World*, 11.
2. Schmemann, *For the Life of the World*, 14.
3. Schmemann, *For the Life of the World*, 14.

the village is a meal. As they near Emmaus, the disciples plead with Jesus not to continue down the road: "But they urged him strongly, saying, 'Stay with us, because it is almost evening and the day is now nearly over.' So he went in to stay with them" (Luke 24:29). The text takes it as a given that to "stay with" the disciples means to dine with them. The very next words, in verse 30, make this clear: "When he was at the table with them . . ." But beyond the implied physical hunger at the end of the walk along the road, the disciples' plea reveals a deeper hunger to remain in Jesus's presence. And this appeal suggests that their conversation has begun to fill the hunger for God that Schmemann described. In fact, we can see in this moment another dimension of the study of theology: *Knowing, loving, and worshiping God is the deepest desire of human beings, and Christian theology is aimed at satisfying this desire.* It would not be quite right, of course, to say that theology (at least in the academic sense) is what we were made for. We were made for communion with God. But theology at its best does indeed help us to know and love God more fully. In this sense, the work of theology is really about connecting us to our highest purpose as human beings.

Perhaps the best-known expression of this purpose is found in St. Augustine's classic work *Confessions*. The book serves as his spiritual autobiography, and it is written as a prayer addressed to God. The very first paragraph of *Confessions* includes a moving account of our deepest longing: "To praise you is the desire of man, a little piece of your creation. You stir man to take pleasure in praising you, because you have made us for yourself, and our heart is restless until it rests in you."[4] The last line was not mere speculation for Augustine, as he had experienced that restlessness firsthand through much of his early adult life. Thus his statement of why God created us frames the life story that he tells in *Confessions*. While he sought for many years to satisfy that hunger with the wrong things, he was ultimately disappointed by all of them. It was only when he was finally willing to lay down

---

4. Augustine, *Confessions* 1.1 (Chadwick, 3).

all other claims on his heart and yield to God's good will that he found what he was looking for. "Suddenly," he recalled,

> it had become sweet to me to be without the sweets of folly. What I once feared to lose was now a delight to dismiss. You turned them out and entered to take their place, pleasanter than any pleasure. . . . Already my mind was free of "the biting cares" of place-seeking, of desire for gain, of wallowing in self-indulgence, of scratching the itch of lust. And I was now talking with you, Lord my God, my radiance, my wealth, and my salvation.[5]

Augustine's insight into human purpose is echoed widely throughout the Christian tradition. Let's look at just a few examples. In her classic work *Revelations of Divine Love*, Julian of Norwich highlights the futility of seeking satisfaction in created goods:

> This is the reason why we do not feel complete ease in our hearts and souls: we look here for satisfaction in things which are so trivial, where there is no rest to be found, and do not know our God who is almighty, all wise, all good; he is rest itself. God wishes to be known, and is pleased that we should rest in Him; for all that is below him does nothing to satisfy us; and this is why, until all that is made seems as nothing, no soul can be at rest.[6]

Christian catechetical works throughout the centuries provide further helpful examples. The very first question of the "Westminster Larger Catechism," a document produced in the seventeenth century for teaching the Christian faith, is about human purpose: "What is the chief and highest end of man?" The answer: "Man's chief and highest end is to glorify God, and fully to enjoy him forever."[7] Another beautiful expression is found in the current *Catechism of the Catholic Church*: "The desire for God is written in the human heart, because man is created by God and for God; and

---

5. Augustine, *Confessions* 9.1 (Chadwick, 155).

6. Julian, *Revelations of Divine Love* [Long Text] 5 (Spearing, 47).

7. "Westminster Larger Catechism" Question 1 (*Book of Catechisms*, 153).

God never ceases to draw man to himself. Only in God will he find the truth and happiness he never stops searching for."[8]

Across these various examples, we can see three common features. First, the primary end for which we were created is to love, praise, and glorify God. We are creatures who have been made for communion with God, and the proper mode of that communion is loving worship. Second, we long to fulfill this purpose, and this longing is stirred within us by God our creator. It is true that human beings are often not consciously aware of the proper object of their desire. Augustine eventually realized that the desires he had felt for fame and pleasure were really expressions of his deepest longing for God—but he had not recognized that while he was pursuing these other goals. Part of the experience of sinful creatures in a fallen world is misreading what we most want, and thus we seek to satisfy our desire for the Creator with created goods. But as Augustine found out, these things do not really deliver any lasting fulfillment. We often get a sense of this dissatisfaction, a feeling that we are looking for something we haven't found, even before any conscious encounter with God. But once we find it—or, even better, once we are found—we know. And that leads to a third common feature: the experience of fulfilling that purpose is deep and abiding joy. The various words used above to describe this, such as rest, delight, and happiness, capture the sense that we were made for joyful union with God.

With all of this in mind, the question for us to take up is this: How can the study of theology direct us to the fulfillment of this highest purpose? If God is not only our source but also our highest end, how do we approach theology so as to direct us toward communion with God? We can begin with an answer so obvious that it is implied in the question, and yet it still needs to be said. Theology must always remain centered on God. It is increasingly common for theologians to describe their discipline in a wide variety of ways. Some see it as a lens with which to examine the social, economic, and political patterns of the world. Some prefer to view theology as a means of discovering and narrating

8. *Catechism of the Catholic Church* para. 27.

identity. Others understand the work of theology as developing a set of skills to be used for making a difference in the world. And it can be all of these things, rightly understood. One can read Augustine, for example, as pursuing some of these goals in his own theological work. But theology is first and foremost about God. If God's nature and activity are not at the heart of theological study, the distinct contribution that theologians have to make is lost. Even more, if the primary purpose of theology is understood as seeking some particular outcome in the world rather than knowing and loving God, then we have lost our way.

There are two questions that we can ask of any text or theological conversation that will help keep us on course. The first is: How does this relate to the nature or the activity of the Triune God? If the entire discussion operates on the plane of human activity, then we are really not in the territory of theology. Even when we are exploring a topic within theology that rightly focuses on creatures (such as theological anthropology), we are primarily interested in how those creatures relate to God. We must always be attentive to whether substantial attention is given to the God we worship as we go about our work. The second question is this: Does the apostolic witness to God's activity in Jesus make any significant difference in the discussion at hand? Here we recall the central point of chapter 1: Christian theology begins with testimony to God's action. As we saw in that chapter, the particular testimony of the apostolic community to what God has done in Jesus gives rise to theological reflection. If you are reading a text or listening to a lecture and you find that the central claims do not depend in any way on the life, death, and resurrection of Jesus, then it is worth asking if you are really encountering Christian theology. It will not do simply to apply theological language to insights derived from other disciplines. Rather, the particular content of Christian proclamation—centered in the crucified and risen Jesus—must shape the discourse in a substantial way.

I must be clear at this point I am not rejecting the value of interdisciplinary conversations between theology and other areas of study. Reading texts and talking with experts in other disciplines can yield a great deal of fruit in understanding the world that God has made. But this kind of interaction is only truly interdisciplinary if theology proper is part of the conversation. Conversations across disciplines cannot be a one-way street; both must contribute and receive insights appropriate to their respective domains of knowledge. If Christian theology is to contribute to an interdisciplinary dialogue, then the content of divine revelation must shape that dialogue in a meaningful way. In fact, focused attention on the revelatory acts of God is precisely what theology as a discipline has to contribute. In this light, interdisciplinary conversations can be extraordinarily helpful in identifying points of contact between special divine revelation (the concern of theology) and our experience as examined through the various other disciplines. It is always worth asking, therefore, what particular contribution the theological partner in interdisciplinary dialogue is offering.

So the first way that the work of theology points us toward the fulfillment of our highest purpose is in its content: theology is about God. A second way is that it stirs our innate hunger for God. It is important, then, to welcome and pay careful attention to this longing as we go about our theological studies. As we have already seen, that hunger is already present in all of us. But we do not always recognize it for what it is. We can convince ourselves that our immediate and transitory desires for created things will ultimately satisfy us, ignoring what we really want and need at the core of our souls. But turning to the study of theology can be an important step in the right direction. It can, so to speak, begin to scratch an itch that we didn't realize that we had. You might find that you desire more and more to learn about the God who has encountered us in Jesus. This can show up in all sorts of ways: reading beyond what is assigned, talking about what you're learning with friends and family in your spare time, and seeking out your teachers for conversations outside of class. When we approach theology as a means of deeper communion with God, it tends to make us want more. In our own way, we will find ourselves urging Jesus to stay with us longer, as the disciples did when they reached Emmaus.

It is of course true, as we have emphasized throughout this discussion, that learning *about* God is not the same as knowing God. We should thus distinguish between the stirring of the soul for God that we have in mind here and mere intellectual interest in theology. Plenty of people who have no particular faith commitments find the Christian intellectual tradition to be interesting. They set out to learn more about it, and often this takes the shape of formal study such as pursuing a degree in theology. Such students often find that they are stirred intellectually and seek out more reading and conversation. And we must be clear that this can be a good thing, particularly if the student is at some level open to the genuine possibility of the truth of Christianity. Such seeds can sprout into eternal fruit. But if that possibility is ruled out from the outset and the study of the Christian tradition is nothing more than an intellectual interest from a detached observer, the deepest need of the soul will remain unmet.

How can we tell the difference? It is a question worth asking, particularly since our hunger for God includes the cognitive dimension. We are called to love God with our minds as well as our hearts and souls (Matt 22:37). The problem emerges when the study of theology is nothing more than an exercise of intellectual curiosity. If a student sets up a barrier between the object of study and the deepest parts of the self, then that person's hunger cannot be filled. To be more precise, the human will must be laid open before God for theology to do its proper work (more on this below). It is not too much to say that the submission of the will to God is the key difference between theology that is pursued as a hobby and theology that bears genuine spiritual fruit. The surest way to keep theological study from touching one's deepest hunger is to guard the will. If we insist from the outset, consciously or unconsciously, to hold onto our desires unchecked, then the work of theology cannot reach its most significant goal.

At this point, someone might raise a fair and important question: What about those times in our studies when we do not consciously feel our hunger for God stirred? If we find ourselves in a season where we feel unmotivated to complete assignments or come to class, should we despair? The answer is a resounding no. It is not at all uncommon to experience periods where our passion for our studies seems to pale in comparison to other interests. This can especially be the case when we find ourselves drowning in a sea of long reading assignments, endless papers to write, and exams that are approaching all too quickly. In these times, it's not especially surprising that students feel the desire to escape these responsibilities and do something else.

What we feel in such seasons is probably a combination of inertia and the pull of lesser desires. You may recall from physics that inertia is the tendency for objects at rest to remain at rest (and for objects in motion to remain in motion). When growth toward a positive goal requires a measure of discipline and hard work, it can be hard to get ourselves moving in that direction even if we believe that the goal is good. And there is no getting around the fact that this kind of discipline is necessary for theology to bear fruit. But it's also the case that when we feel that desire to remain at rest— to avoid the hard work—the attraction of lesser goods becomes comparatively stronger. We have all felt this to some degree; for example, when the idea of watching television seems so much more appealing when we have a paper coming due. There is no getting around the fact that there are times when we simply need to press ahead and do the work. By holding ourselves accountable (or inviting others to help hold us accountable) to complete assignments even when we would rather be doing something else, we open the door to genuine growth. And then we often find that inertia begins to work in our favor. Objects in motion tend to stay in motion; in a similar way, the completion of one paper or project can energize us to tackle the next. And that is when we are apt to find that our theological studies are stirring our souls again.

A third way in which theology directs us toward our ultimate purpose is found in the response called forth by theological study. As we anticipated in our previous point, Christian theology is aimed at the submission of the will to God. While theology deals directly with claims of knowledge about God's nature and activity, that knowledge is not meant to be received passively.

God has revealed himself through particular actions in the world in order that we might respond. And that response, as we saw exemplified in Augustine's story above, is the yielding of our desires to God's desires for us. This does not come easily for us as human beings, and we must always remember that God knows and desires our good—even in ways that we may not be able initially to see. In fact, our ability to see and pursue what is genuinely good for us is notoriously unreliable, which is why submission to God's will is so important.

As we saw at the outset of this chapter, Schmemann recognized that our lives are marked by hunger for the good. And because every created good is only good insofar as it participates in God's eternal and unchanging goodness, our desires in this life are rooted in a fundamental longing for God. But we are fallen creatures in a fallen world, and we have a remarkable tendency to chase after the wrong things. Even at the level of everyday life, we can immediately think of ways in which we pursue false goods (or pursue genuine goods in disordered ways). False goods are just what they sound like: things that we think will be good for us that actually harm us. For example, in a moment of deep frustration or impatience with another person, it may appear that lashing out at them with angry words will make us feel better. But if you've ever given into that temptation, then you have likely learned that it is not satisfying at all (and very likely causes damage in the relationship). Sometimes the things we seek are truly good when received in the right manner, but we misuse them in ways that distort their goodness. Food is a genuine good when it is eaten to nourish our bodies, give thanks to God, and enjoy fellowship with other people. But when we overindulge in food to try to ease a spiritual or emotional problem, then something has become disordered. The desires for these false or disordered goods can be very strong, as we have all learned from experience. So the submission of the will is not by any means a simple matter.

The fundamental problem, then, is that there is a gap between what we feel we want and what is truly good for us. We are rightly inclined to move toward what we think will benefit us in some way, but our desires often lead us away from what is truly good. And the only help for this problem is the God who both perfectly knows what is good and desires the best for us. When we keep in mind that God knows and wills our good, then we see why the process of conforming our wills to God's will is so important. While our particular desires often lead us in the wrong direction, God's good will for us guides us toward what we most deeply need. The process of surrender, difficult as it often is, is necessary for us to get where we were meant to go. And as Christians have long recognized, prayer is at the heart of that process.

Prayer, at its core, is a means of aligning our wills with God's will. In the presence of God, we ask for—and find—the strength to trust that God truly knows what we most want and need. That God-enabled trust is demonstrated when we lay aside those things that are incompatible with God's will, even at the very moment we may desire them most strongly. At the core of the Lord's Prayer is a petition for God's will to be done. And while that petition is certainly a request for God's will to be done in the world at large, it is also a plea for the strength to do God's will in one's own life. Jesus not only taught his disciples to pray this model prayer, but he also demonstrated it in his own prayer life. The way the Gospel of Matthew narrates Jesus's time of prayer in Gethsemane, the night before his death, is instructive for us. He first prays in these words: "My Father, if it is possible, let this cup pass from me, yet not what I want but what you want" (Matt 26:39). The cup he speaks of is the suffering and death that await him. In his prayer, Jesus acknowledges the desire of his human will to avoid this suffering. Yet the crucial moment is the submission of his human will ("what I want") to the divine will he shares with the Father ("what you want"). This provides a glimpse of what all prayer is ultimately about: the aligning of the human will with the divine will. As Matthew tells the story, Jesus prays in similar words two more times, and in the second, he echoes the line "your will be done" from the Lord's Prayer (Matt 26:42; 6:10).[9] In the

---

9. The echo is present in the Greek text.

Gethsemane prayer, then, Jesus is opening the way for our own prayers to help conform our desires to God's.

At this point we might ask what this discussion of prayer has to do with the work of theology. Here we must recall our reflections from chapter 2 on the essential connection between theology and prayer. We saw there that the work of theology is best conceived as part of our prayer lives. Knowing more about God and God's activity is a means of knowing God more intimately. In that sense, the work of Christian theology draws us deeper into communion with God. Now we are in a position to make a critical connection as to why that is: theology is a discipline that enables us to learn God's will. Because so much of our lives is spent pursuing goals that lead us away from the communion with God we were created for, we need focused means of learning a better way to live. That is what theology offers, precisely because its subject is God's nature, God's activity, and our place within God's creative intention. Sustained attention on these matters therefore sharpens our sense of who God is and what God wants for us. The work of theology can then become a key part of a prayer life that is aimed at aligning our desires to that vision. In the process, we find that we are in deepening communion with the very good that we have been seeking our whole lives. This is the same experience that prompted the disciples on the Emmaus road to beg Jesus to stay with them longer.

One final note should be sounded on the topic of theology and the submission of the will. Unfortunately, theologians can lose their way and try to turn theology into something it was never meant to be: a means of rationalizing ends that they already want. I suspect this is not a conscious choice on their part. Rather, we can want so badly for others to take certain social or political stances that we read those stances into the source material of Christian theology. Rather than prompting us to lay down our wills, then, theological discourse becomes a way of reinforcing what we already desire. At its worst, this can foster a kind of idolatry, where we proclaim a god made in our own image. By contrast, when we approach theology in a proper posture, we will find that we are sometimes surprised by what God's will demands of us. If you find at the end of your formal program of study in theology that you want all the same things that you wanted when you began, then it may be a good time for careful self-examination. Theology is aimed at the submission of our desires to God's will.

Finally, a fourth way that studying theology connects us to our purpose as human beings is that it offers a joyful glimpse of what awaits us in the life to come. We saw in chapter 2 that joy is one mark of theology done in the company of God. This joy is the natural fruit of experiencing communion with God in the present life. But it also is a foretaste of what we will experience fully in eternity. As our studies in theology point us to the God we were made to love and worship, we recognize that the fullness of our desire for God cannot be completely satisfied in this life. We are simultaneously aware that we were made for God and that the complete fulfillment of that purpose awaits us in the resurrection life. "For now we see only a reflection, as in a mirror," the apostle Paul reminds us, "but then we will see face to face. Now I know only in part; then I will know fully, even as I have been fully known" (1 Cor 13:12).

There are two levels on which the study of theology points us to the life to come. The first and more narrow level is eschatology, one of the central topics or "loci" of Christian theology. Eschatology refers to the study of Christian hope, and it includes such matters as the return of Jesus, the resurrection of the dead, the final judgment, and eternal life with God. So when we devote explicit attention to eschatology in our reading, writing, and conversation, we are reflecting directly on the life with God that awaits us. There is plenty, to be sure, that is unknown about our future (as Paul acknowledges in the First Corinthians text above.) But Christian hope rests on the promises of God that have been given in divine revelation, and these are the proper subject matter of eschatology. Still, it is not only the study of eschatology that draws our hearts and minds to the fulfillment of our hope. The second and broader level on which this happens involves the entire range of Christian doctrine. As we explore the nature and actions of God in all of the loci of Christian theology, we are assured that this is a God who is faithful and whose promises are sure. The entire saving work of the Triune God draws us toward the joy of the life to come in his presence.

And that eternal life with God is a life of worship. We get many glimpses of this in Scripture, as the creatures who attend God in the heavenly court are depicted as continually praising God.[10] In that light, we can see that the worship that the church offers to God in this life is an anticipation of heaven. When we gather as a community of faith to worship the Triune God, we are getting a taste of the joy of eternal life. This is, in fact, a major theme of Schmemann's *For the Life of the World*, the book that framed the opening of this chapter. Schmemann focuses on the Eucharist in particular as a journey in which we ascend to the joy of heaven in the midst of time and space.[11] It is fitting, then, to see that the journey on the Emmaus road culminates in the breaking of the bread with the risen Jesus. The crucial place of that meal in the narrative reminds us of the essential connection between theological conversation and the practices of Christian worship. In the next chapter, we turn to explore this connection directly.

10. Isa 6, Ps 148, and Rev 4 are notable examples.
11. See chapter 2 of Schmemann, *For the Life of the World*, in particular.

Chapter 5: The Breaking of the Bread

In the Christian tradition, there is a longstanding principle known by its Latin phrasing: *lex orandi, lex credendi*. The basic meaning of this phrase is "the law of prayer is the law of belief." Prayer in this context does not mean one's private spontaneous prayers from the heart but rather the common prayer or worship of the church. So the idea at the heart of the principle is that there is a correspondence between the beliefs of the church and the way that it worships and prays—between theology and liturgy, we could say. The prayers, songs, readings, and practices that make up the church's worship life reflect the same commitments of belief that we find summarized in Christian creeds and confessions. Knowledge of God's nature and activity shapes faithful worship, and faithful worship deepens and refines our knowledge of God.

On the Emmaus road, Jesus had opened the Scriptures to the disciples so that they could understand the actions of God that had unfolded in the death and resurrection of the messiah. That theological conversation continued into town, where (as we saw in the last chapter) the two disciples begged Jesus to come inside and stay with them. As they sat down at the table, Jesus took four specific actions with the bread: he took it, blessed it, broke it, and gave it to the disciples (Luke 24:30). Luke's first audience, and generations of Christians down through the centuries since, would recognize in these four movements the pattern of a central act of Christian worship: the sacrament of the Eucharist. Not only did the theological conversation give way to the breaking of the bread, but it was in this meal that the disciples recognized that the stranger was in fact Jesus (v. 31). This point gets reinforced at the end of the narrative, when the two disciples report to the other disciples "how he had been made known to them in the breaking of the bread" (v. 35).

The Emmaus story thus connects the disciples' increasing knowledge of Jesus with a central act of worship. This connection helps us to see yet another dimension of the study of theology: *we come to know God in the practices of Christian worship.* This is obviously not to say that there is no place for the sorts of things we do in academic theology, such as reading, writing, and conversation. The book you are reading now is an invitation to precisely these practices for the purpose of knowing God more deeply. It is to say that our reading, writing, and conversations bear fruit when they are ordered to and shaped by regular participation in the worshiping community of faith. Like the disciples at Emmaus, we too will come to see in the breaking of the bread that Jesus is with us—and has been with us on our journey even when we didn't realize it. Sustained and attentive participation in worship will enable our studies to lead us closer to God. You may also find, as generations of students have found before you, that theological studies enhance the experience of worship. You will likely see new dimensions of meaning as you receive the sacraments, sing songs of worship, and join with the church in other practices of worship.

The unity of worship and theology is emphasized in an interesting way in the *Catechism of the Catholic Church.* In the section on the structure of the Catholic Mass, the document notes that there are "two great parts that form a fundamental unity": the liturgy of the Word and the liturgy of the Eucharist. These parts "together form 'one single act of worship.'"[1] The Catechism then appeals to a remarkable precedent for this unity: "Is this not the same movement as the Paschal meal of the risen Jesus with his disciples? Walking with them he explained the Scriptures to them; sitting with them at table 'he took bread, blessed and

1. *Catechism of the Catholic Church* para. 1346.

broke it, and gave it to them."[2] The footnote for this paragraph points us to Luke 24:13–35, the Emmaus narrative at the heart of our study. The point seems to be that the movement of the Eucharistic liturgy is the movement of the Emmaus story. And theology, exemplified here in Jesus's instruction to the disciples, is part of the movement of the worshiping community. The connection between theological reflection on the Scriptures and the practices of worship is therefore signaled in our Emmaus story, as highlighted by a major catechetical text.

As we consider the correspondence between worship and theology, it is important to clarify what we mean by the word worship. For our purposes, at least, I have in mind the gathered Christian community joining in particular recognized patterns of worship. It is common these days to think of a hike in the woods or coffee with a friend as acts of worship. And they can be, in a manner of speaking. It is good and right to think of our entire lives being lived in worship of God's glory, each day throughout the week. In this light, our everyday activities can be lived with attentiveness to God's ongoing presence. Brother Lawrence's *The Practice of the Presence of God* is a classic reflection on this spiritual posture. But while valid, this broad understanding of worship is not all there is to worship. If our only practices of worship are walks in the woods and coffee with friends, then the content of our worship will inevitably become vague and thin.

We need, then, a more particular understanding of worship that helps to prepare us for the broader form of worship in our everyday lives. And this more specific form of worship is our focus in this chapter. Here I have in mind the regular and intentional worship practices of the community gathered together in time and space. Across the centuries, Christians have come together on Sunday, the day of Jesus's resurrection, to join in worship. For all of the diversity among Christian communities throughout the world and over time, the basic patterns have remained remarkably similar and recognizable. Believers gather at appointed times to join in prayer, to sing praise to God, to hear the Scriptures read

2. *Catechism of the Catholic Church* para. 1347.

aloud and proclaimed, to celebrate the sacraments, to exchange signs of peace, and so on. Such practices have marked Christian identity for as long as there have been Christians, and we would be unwise to undermine their importance. In these acts of worship, the story of God's particular actions in the world—centered in the life, death, and resurrection of Jesus—are told and retold. Just as theology begins with testimony to God's saving actions in Jesus, so also worship emerges from the church's recognition of who God is and what God has done.

With that in mind, let us turn to explore the nature of the relationship between Christian worship and Christian theology in greater detail. It is worth noting that the principle of *lex orandi, lex credendi* moves in both directions. That is, it is the case both that theology shapes worship and that worship shapes theology. It might be tempting to imagine that the Christian community first worked out its beliefs and then developed liturgies that reflected those beliefs. But in reality there was mutual interaction among those expressions of the church's life: the community of faith was worshiping continually over the centuries when key doctrines were prayerfully developed and refined. The language and thought forms of the liturgy undoubtedly shaped the ways that Christian belief was articulated. The confessing church has always been the worshiping church.

From the other side, the content of divine revelation both provides the raw material for Christian worship and sets its boundaries. It is true that there are instances where a particular liturgical form is part of the content of divine revelation—Jesus teaching the Lord's Prayer to his disciples or instituting the Lord's Supper are two clear examples. And those forms can shape theological reflection in illuminating ways, such as when we draw conclusions about prayer in general from studying the Lord's Prayer. Furthermore, as we will see below, the response of the community of faith in worship is a key part of the larger movement of divine revelation. But it would be a mistake to suppose that the direction of movement is always from the liturgy to theology. One of the key purposes of creeds, confessions, and statements of faith is to clarify the beliefs of the Christian faith so that the church can worship faithfully. We get a hint of this in the word "orthodoxy," which generally means both sound belief and faithful worship. So the whole body of apostolic witness to God's saving activity, centered in the Scriptures, shapes the patterns of Christian worship. In this way, we respond in worship by glorifying the same Triune God who creates, redeems, and sanctifies us.

As we proceed, we will see this two-way movement of the *lex orandi, lex credendi* principle. We begin by considering some specific ways that worship influences theology, and then we will turn to explore how theology shapes worship. Our Emmaus text gives us a good look at one central way that worship is necessary for theology. As emphasized at the end of the passage, Jesus was made known to the two disciples in the breaking of the bread. They did not recognize Jesus while they were talking with him about the Scriptures along the road, but they only realized it was him when they were at the table with him. This is a remarkably poignant clue about how we come to know God: the habit and posture of worship enables us to see God. Theological study enables us to learn a great deal about what Christians believe about God. But reading books and listening to lectures is not enough to *know* God. Worship, when we yield our hearts in praise of God and in allegiance to God, is when we really begin to see.

At this point we need to consider a question that the Emmaus text naturally invites: Why couldn't the disciples recognize Jesus at first? The two uses of the passive voice in this narrative are both vague and intriguing: "Their eyes were kept from recognizing him" in verse 16 and "their eyes were opened" in verse 31. The text simply does not tell us what or who was doing the keeping and the opening. There seem to be at least two reasonable possibilities. One possibility is that the passive voice is an indirect way of referring to divine action. That is, it was God who was keeping their eyes from recognizing Jesus and opening their eyes at the table. This would enable the disciples' experience to unfold in just the way that God intended, in order to instruct those two followers of Jesus as well as the later generations who would hear their story.

Another possibility is that the disciples' own spiritual posture was responsible for what they were able to see. On this reading, their own doubt about the testimony from the empty tomb (v. 22–24) and their slowness to believe (v. 25) was what kept their eyes from recognizing Jesus. But their active welcoming of Jesus (v. 29) and reception of the bread he offered them (v. 30) opened their eyes to see that Jesus had been with them all along.

While these two readings of the story differ on who closed and opened the disciples' eyes, they agree on the main point: that it was in the breaking of the bread that their eyes were opened. And even on the second interpretation, where God is not actively disengaging and engaging the senses of the disciples, it is still the case that God has created the conditions in which Jesus can be recognized.[3] Either way, then, the text seems to suggest that God has designed us in such a way that we recognize him in a posture of worship. This aligns well with what we saw in our last chapter; namely, that human beings were made to find eternal joy in loving and worshiping God. In that posture, our spiritual senses—most centrally the ability to see God—function as they should. We see most clearly when we are doing what we were created to do.

But how does this activation of our spiritual senses in worship shape our theological work? We can think of theology as disciplined reflection on what God has revealed to us about himself and his purposes. As we have seen, that reflection begins with testimony to particular divine actions. As we respond in a posture of attentive worship, we see even more clearly who God is and what God has done. In other words, part of the process of divine revelation is Jesus being made known to us in the breaking of the bread. The work of theology is aimed at clarifying and articulating

---

3. This is, of course, not the only New Testament text where the risen Jesus is unrecognized by some of his followers. A very interesting passage for comparison is John 20:11–18, where Mary Magdalene meets the risen Jesus outside the tomb but does not recognize him at first. Notably, in that text Mary recognizes Jesus when he says her name (v. 16). While Luke 24 and John 20 perhaps suggest that there was something new and different about the resurrected body of Jesus, these and other resurrection accounts in the Gospels make it clear that he was ultimately recognizable.

what we have seen in this unfolding revelation. And that work must continue in a posture of attentive worship. As theologians we read and discuss Scripture, as well as other materials—creeds and confessions, the classic writings of the Christian tradition, liturgies, hymnody, and so on—in order to immerse ourselves in the church's reception of divine revelation. We do all this in a spirit of worship and prayer, with the aim of drawing close to the God who has given us these treasures. In this posture, we come to see more and more of God's nature and purposes. And ultimately, we speak, write, and sing theology out of that experience of divine initiative and human response.

The reference above to liturgies as a source for theological reflection leads us to a second way in which worship shapes theology. The actual materials of worship are rich resources for the work of theology. These include particular liturgies of the churches, the prayers and actions by which we celebrate the sacraments, and songs of worship. If it is true that the worship of the church is part of the unfolding of divine revelation, then the words and actions of that worship deserve the attention of theologians as they go about their work. The prayers and songs of the church in worship are different from other theological writings in one respect; namely, that they are generally addressed to God rather than to other people.[4] But because these prayers and songs recount the saving acts of God in detail, and aim to glorify the God who saves us, they are treasures for those interested in precisely these matters. Carefully reflecting on the materials used to worship God can help to clarify the nature and activity of the God who is worshiped.

There is a key premise underlying this mining of particular prayers or hymns in the work of theology. The premise is that every act of worship says something about the God who is worshiped. (This is, of course, true of misdirected worship as well. If some god other than the Triune God of our salvation is being worshiped, the

---

4. There are, of course, exceptions to this in the form of theological classics that are addressed to God. St. Augustine's *Confessions* and St. Catherine of Siena's *The Dialogue* are two important examples. Ultimately, these exceptions reinforce the deep connection between theology and praise that is at the heart of this chapter.

forms of worship will make the specific nature of the idolatry clear.) When we examine sacramental prayers carefully, for example, we will see specific works of God recounted; the very works that are received and celebrated in the sacraments. When we consider the lyrics of a song of worship, we will be able to identify the particular attributes of God that merit the praise of the community of faith. While the products of explicitly theological work—books, articles, and the like—are different from the materials of worship, they are celebrating the same attributes and actions of God. And thus the books and articles that theologians write and read are enriched deeply by interaction with the materials of worship.[5]

A third way in which worship shapes theology has to do with the purpose of our theological work. At one level, as we've seen, the ultimate aim of theology is our union with God. For our own highest good, we seek to draw near to the God who has come near to us. At another level, though, the purpose of our theological work is not centered on ourselves at all. That is, we read, write, and discuss theology to glorify God. These two purposes of theology are not at all incompatible. In fact, it is only in a posture of praise and grateful reception of God's grace that we are even able to draw near to God. The means of deeper communion with God are the forms by which we offer joyful and thankful attention to God: prayer, receiving the sacraments, worship, and so on. To put the matter directly, our highest good is the glorification of God. It is of course true that there may be any number of narrower and more specific goals as we go about the study of theology—to clarify how the atoning work of Jesus should be preached, for example, or to identify the various aspects of the meaning of baptism. But even as we go about these more immediate tasks, the ultimate aim of pursuing them is to draw nearer to God in a posture of worship.

Another way of making this point is that theology and worship are linked precisely as means of loving God. Elsewhere I have described the love of God as delighting in and moving toward the perfect good that God is.[6] Love for God involves rejoicing in the

5. One beautiful example is Geoffrey Wainwright's monumental *Doxology*.
6. Koskela, "What Is Love?"

love, mercy, justice, and power of God as well as in the actions of God in the world that display these attributes. Yet it also involves a movement on our part toward the goodness of God that has been shown to us. "As he who called you is holy," 1 Pet 1:15–16 contends, "be holy yourselves in all your conduct, for it is written, 'You shall be holy, for I am holy.'"[7] Though it is not particularly common to think of it this way, the work of theology should really be understood in this light. We love God through our theological study by naming and delighting in the goodness of God, which is reflected in the particulars of what we read, write, and discuss. And we also love God by moving toward God's goodness, which we celebrate in our theological work. A treatise on the person and work of the Holy Spirit or an article on the Trinitarian processions is ultimately meaningful to the degree that it helps the community of faith draw nearer to the God that is described. In this respect, theology is truly a means of worship.

Alas, recognizing the proper aim of the study of theology forces us to acknowledge how often it is pursued for other ends. To put the matter bluntly, when we approach theology primarily as a means of advancing a career, something has gone desperately wrong. This can certainly happen among professional theologians, particularly when their efforts are aimed mainly at raising their own public profile. If the measure of a theologian is found in book sales, lectureship invitations, and prime academic jobs rather than in the glorification of God, then the very purpose of our discipline has been distorted. When those goals become primary, then one will be inclined to write or say whatever the audience of the moment wants to hear rather than the truths about God and the world that need to be heard. In that light, remembering the purpose of theology can help to keep the content of theology on track. Theology that aims to glorify God will be concerned to speak faithfully to what is always true about God.

The temptation to approach theology primarily as a means of career advancement is, of course, not only a temptation for

---

7. This New Testament text is echoing an idea that repeats throughout Leviticus: 11:44, 45; 19:2; and 20:7 are examples.

professional theologians. Students pursuing formal theological studies can fall into the same pattern. If someone's *only* consideration in beginning a degree program is to meet a denominational requirement or to secure a job in ministry, then it becomes harder to see the work in that program as a means of glorifying God. This will show up in all sorts of unhealthy ways: that student will tend to write assignments that reflect only what the professor wants to hear, shortcuts will be taken in reading assignments, and the academic work will be distanced from (or, worse, will replace) the student's own spiritual growth. If one begins the study of theology with the idea that the work is merely a means to a professional end, then one's work will reflect that belief.

As a theology professor, I recognize that this all may seem hopelessly naïve. I fully acknowledge that very few people have the luxury of ignoring practical considerations when considering a degree program. The reality is that denominational requirements and job prospects are a significant factor for most people in beginning a course of study, particularly at the seminary level. The key is in how the actual work of theology is viewed during the course of one's journey. For example, denominational requirements about degrees in theology are often in place because of the inherent value of theological education for the health of the church. It is important for church leaders to be committed to loving God with their hearts, minds, and souls—the very core of a good theological education. Many people would not be able to justify taking years of their life to commit to a degree program if it were not a practical necessity for their vocation. But in those cases, the work of reading and writing in those years can still be treated as a means of loving and serving God. By contrast, someone who views the work as nothing more than steps on a career ladder will be rather unlikely to encounter theology as a means of glorifying and drawing nearer to God. At the beginning of your journey of theological study, it is good to examine carefully your reasons for getting started. If your reasons are exclusively focused on yourself, then this is a good time to consider how your work can be a means of glorifying God. Doing so will make the journey much more fulfilling for you. Somewhat ironically, we often need to get our attention off of ourselves and onto God truly to help ourselves move forward.

So far, we've been examining ways that worship influences theological study. Now we shift to consider how theology shapes our worship. We will start at the macro level, where the fruit of the church's theological reflection guides the formal patterns of worship. That is, our theological convictions help us to worship with words, imagery, and practices that are faithful to God's self-revelation. This is true both of the broad traditions of Christian worship shared by the various churches and of the liturgies of the particular denominations.

At the broadest level, the core Christian doctrines that were refined in the first few centuries of the church's life have shaped the patterns of Christian worship ever since. To take just one example: Is it proper for Christians to pray only to God the Father, or is it appropriate to address prayer to all of the Trinitarian persons? The answer is the latter—Christians can and do pray to God the Father, God the Son, and God the Holy Spirit. And the reason why this is the case takes us back to the fourth century, which was a pivotal time in the development in the doctrine of the Trinity. Theologians gave a lot of attention during that century to the persons of the Trinity. The focus was initially centered on Jesus (God the Son), and then eventually it shifted to consider the status of the Holy Spirit as well. A key question throughout that time was whether the Son and the Holy Spirit were truly and fully divine—in the sense that God the Father is divine—or whether they could only be considered divine in some lesser sense. The conclusion that emerged, stated most prominently in the Nicene-Constantinopolitan Creed of AD 381, was that the Son and the Holy Spirit were fully and truly God as the Father is God.

This conclusion had significant implications for Christian worship. For one thing, it helped the church to avoid the charge of idolatry. Christians had worshipped Jesus from the very beginning. If Jesus were anything less than fully divine, then worshiping him would be deeply problematic.[8] Another implication is

8. This was a significant issue in the Arian controversy in the fourth

that it is entirely appropriate to address prayer and worship to each of the three persons of the Trinity. This was a major theme of a classic fourth-century work, *On the Holy Spirit* by St. Basil the Great. In that treatise, Basil argued forcefully that the Holy Spirit should be ranked together with God the Father and God the Son. He appealed to Jesus's command to the disciples in Matt 28 to baptize in the name of the Father, of the Son, and of the Holy Spirit as evidence against those who would suggest that the Spirit is inferior to the Father and the Son.[9] Basil also argued that the works of the Holy Spirit reveal the Spirit's full divinity, since those actions are proper only to God and not to creatures.[10] He concluded by asserting that it is appropriate for Christians to glorify God the Father together with the Son and with the Spirit.[11] The preposition "with"—and prepositions are very important to Basil's argument in this work—indicates the full equality of the Trinitarian persons in Christian teaching and worship. To put the matter sharply, the theological conviction of the full divinity of the three persons of the Trinity grounds the practice of praying directly to all three persons.

Such large-scale examples of Christian doctrine shaping worship and prayer generally hold across the various church traditions. But within particular denominations and churches, great care is also taken to ensure that the words and actions of worship align with the teaching of those churches. There typically are specific structures in each denomination[12] to review, revise, and approve

---

century, given Arius's contention that the Son was a creature rather than the uncreated God. If one worships the Son and at the same time claims that Son is created, then it is very difficult to see how that worship avoids idolatry. See Pelikan, *Emergence of the Catholic Tradition*, 198–200; Wilken, *Spirit of Early Christian Thought*, 82–85.

9. Basil, *On the Holy Spirit* 10.24–26 (Hildebrand, 55–57).

10. Basil, *On the Holy Spirit* 19.48–50 (Hildebrand, 84–87).

11. Basil, *On the Holy Spirit* 27.65–68 (Hildebrand, 103–8).

12. I recognize that the word "denomination" is mainly used in Protestant churches, and my argument here also applies to other ecclesial traditions. I alternate in this paragraph between "church" (which can give the wrong impression that I mean local congregations) and "denomination" (which can give

worship resources for use in local churches. These structures vary from church to church, but often there is a designated commission or committee that is tasked with the responsibility to review and propose any revisions to liturgical resources. Usually, those proposals then need to be approved by the primary decision-making body in that denomination—for example, the General Assembly in a Presbyterian denomination or the General Conference in a Methodist denomination. In most churches, significant revisions of worship materials do not happen especially frequently. But when they do undertake that task, the people involved in the process work carefully to align worship resources closely with the doctrines of that church. These doctrines are typically expressed formally in articles of religion, confessions of faith, and the like. Such written expressions of church teaching thus serve as important guides for the actual content of worship.

Theology also influences worship at the micro level; that is, at the level of those who are participating in worship. The more the specifics of Christian beliefs are taught in the local congregation, the more people will recognize and appreciate the riches of the church's worship. Newcomers to church often find worship to be captivating but mysterious. There is a great deal that Christians say, sing, and do in the course of a service that people may not initially understand. In this light, the process of catechesis—or teaching the basics of the faith—is a crucial part of Christian initiation. It is not only that people need to understand the beliefs held by the community they are considering joining (though that certainly is important). It is also important for people to learn these basics in order to comprehend what is happening in worship and to appreciate that worship in greater depth.

As you move deeper into your study of theology, you will likely find that your own appreciation for the beauty of Christian worship will increase. Even for those who know the basics, there is always

the wrong impression that I only have Protestants in mind) for lack of a better term. Even the phrase "ecclesial tradition" is not quite right, since an ecclesial tradition such as the Reformed tradition or the Wesleyan tradition has many denominational bodies within it.

more to learn and take in. The treasures of the church's music, prayers, and sacramental practices are inexhaustible in their beauty and power. Students of theology often find that the lyrics of songs sung in worship or passages of Scripture read aloud now hit them in different ways. With the new lenses their studies have offered, they recognize echoes from Scripture in songs they have long known. They see the significance of specific lines from the prayers and words of institution at communion. The entire shape and structure of a worship service begins to make more sense than it did before. This is a development to be welcomed and embraced.

Of course, newly acquired knowledge can cut both ways. Newer students often begin to exercise their developing theological muscles by critiquing a great deal of what they see in a worship service. The temptation to point out a questionable exegetical move in a sermon or an inelegant line in a newer worship song is very great at this stage. Indeed, there are times and places to talk about these matters and raise critical questions. But it's important to keep two things in mind if you begin to recognize these tendencies in yourself. First, our focus during worship must always be on God. If you find that what you've learned in classes is making you hypercritical while you are in a worship service, then the remedy is to turn your full attention toward the God who is being worshiped. Second, as we've seen before, sometimes the primary motivation for such critiques is that students want to show off their learning. If you detect somewhere deep down that you're more interested in demonstrating your knowledge than worshiping faithfully, then it is a good time to hold your criticism in check.

It is always worth remembering that our ultimate aim in theology is to see and know God. And as the Emmaus story reminds us, worship practices such as the breaking of the bread enable us to see Jesus in our midst. As soon as we recognize this in the story's climax, of course, a new problem emerges. In verse 31, the very moment the disciples' eyes are opened to recognize Jesus, he vanishes from their sight. As soon as they come to see that their mysterious traveling companion is the risen Jesus himself, he is no longer in their midst. What should we make of this? We move to that question in the chapter to follow.

Chapter 6: The Disappearance

In a story full of surprising twists, the disappearance of Jesus from the table at Emmaus may be the most surprising of all. Toward the end of the narrative, in the breaking of the bread, the two disciples recognize that their mysterious traveling companion is Jesus himself. We might expect at this point that their conversation with Jesus would continue, seasoned with the joy of their newfound understanding. But that is not what happens. "Then their eyes were opened," Luke 24:31 reads, "and they recognized him, and he vanished from their sight." At the very moment their happy reunion is about to commence, Jesus is gone.

What are we to make of this turn of events? We might begin by acknowledging that the risen Jesus is simply different in some ways from how the disciples encountered him before his death. This seems to be a particular point of emphasis in the resurrection stories in Luke and John. We noted in the previous chapter, for example, that the risen Jesus is not initially recognized by Mary Magdalene in John 20 (just as the disciples on the Emmaus road do not recognize Jesus in Luke 24). And again the disciples do not recognize Jesus at first on the shore in John 21:4. There are also multiple stories of Jesus suddenly appearing in the midst of the gathered disciples, including Luke 24:36 (apparently later on the same night of the Emmaus encounter), John 20:19, and John 20:26.

Yet just as the reader may begin to wonder if the disciples are seeing a ghost, both of these Gospel writers include details that make it clear that Jesus is present in the flesh. He eats fish in the presence of the disciples (Luke 24:42–43, and perhaps at least implied in John 21:15). He shows the disciples his hands, feet, and side in Luke 24:39–40, John 20:20, and John 20:24–29—and the last of these accounts makes it clear that Jesus's hands and side still bear the marks of his crucifixion. All of this means that Jesus is present to the disciples in his body, risen from the dead, but he has been transformed in some ways from how he appeared to them before his death. We could reasonably say that in the resurrection the Son's incarnation has moved into a new stage. The risen Jesus appears to his disciples in time and space, and yet his human body now visibly participates in the eternal. And here we find our next cue for the study of theology: *Christian theology is not only about our lives in time; it is also always oriented toward eternity.*

The study of theology is always marked by the tension of the eternal God revealing himself to us in the particularity of time and space. This tension is especially prominent when we understand that we are called to share, by God's grace, in eternity. As we saw in chapter 4, there is a technical term for the specific area of Christian teaching that deals with God's promises for what lies ahead: eschatology. When we explore Christian eschatology, we are taking up matters such as the return of Jesus, the final judgment, and heaven. But even beyond this particular set of topics within Christian doctrine, there is a sense in which all theological study is about the purposes and promises of God for us in eternity. In this chapter, we will consider this eschatological orientation of theology from two specific angles. First, we will examine what this means for our knowledge of God; namely, that it is trustworthy but not complete. Second, we will explore how the ultimate aims of Christian theology go beyond the boundaries of time.

The further you go in your theological journey, the more you will experience a kind of paradox. That is, you will learn more and more about God and the particular ways in which he has worked to draw us closer to him. At the same time, your sense of the mystery and transcendence of God will likely increase. As we read the accounts of God's activity in Scripture and other

Christian writings, we have more to say and proclaim about God's goodness, mercy, and faithfulness. And yet we also find that we are drawn more often to silence in the face of the boundlessness of this God. I want to assure you that this tension—feeling like we know less about God precisely as we are learning more—is an indication that you are moving in the right direction. As St. Augustine put it, "Such ignorance is more religious and devout than any presumption of knowledge. After all, we are talking about God. It says, 'and the Word was God' (John 1:1). We are talking about God; so why be surprised if you cannot grasp it? I mean, if you can grasp it, it isn't God."[1]

This justly famous quotation is worth remembering throughout your theological journey. And yet, we must also be aware of a rather sloppy conclusion that is sometimes drawn from Augustine's point. While it is true that finite creatures cannot fully comprehend the transcendent reality of God, some people are tempted to suggest that we cannot therefore know anything about God. This is a drastic mistake. Christianity rests on the conviction that this God—mysterious, transcendent, ineffable—can get through to us. God is able to reveal truths about his nature and purposes, and God has in fact done so. This has happened through a variety of means: in creation, through human conscience and our innate sense of the divine, through God's particular history with the people of Israel, and ultimately in the incarnation of God the Son in Jesus. That list, in fact, reveals an increasingly clearer picture over time of who God is and what God is doing. The opening lines of Hebrews convey this point particularly well: "Long ago God spoke to our ancestors in many and various ways by the prophets, but in these last days he has spoken to us by a Son" (1:1-2). So in affirming the deep mystery of God, Augustine is not denying all that we have come to know about God through divine revelation. Augustine is one of the greatest teachers of Christian doctrine in the church's history, after all. His point is that these truths about God—truths Augustine spent much of his life communicating— do not exhaust the transcendence of God. For all that we know

1. Augustine, *Sermons on the New Testament* 117.5 (Hill, 211).

by God's gracious self-revelation, we ultimately cannot grasp the fullness of God's reality.

This is why we have to be so careful with how we apply the idea of mystery as we go about our work in Christian theology. It is all too common for students and even faculty in theology to take the idea of God's mystery as a reason to undermine what is known through divine revelation. Sometimes people even appeal to the Augustine quotation above in making this move. Fairly standard claims of historic Christian doctrine are waved away dismissively with sentiments that may initially sound reverent. For example, some may shy away from affirming a full-blooded doctrine of the Trinity because it seems arrogant to suppose that finite human beings can know the transcendent God in such detail. While such comments can sound as if they protect the divine mystery, in reality they reject God's ability to communicate to us truths about himself and to assist us in recognizing those truths. What first might appear as pious intellectual humility ultimately amounts to a denial of God's self-revelation. Furthermore, the example of the doctrine of the Trinity illustrates a further problem with such appeals. The classic doctrine of the Trinity already makes plenty of space for God's mystery. As theologians from the Patristic era affirmed what God has revealed about the eternal relations among the Father, the Son, and the Holy Spirit, for example, they emphatically taught that there is much about the Trinity that God has not given us to know.[2] To put the matter simply: by affirming classic Christian teaching in all of its detail and particularity, we are simultaneously respecting the divine mystery.

Why is it impossible for us to grasp the fullness of God? There are two primary reasons. The first is the asymmetry between God's transcendence and our finitude as creatures. We have focused a good bit in this chapter on the relationship between time, which applies to the realm of creatures, and eternity, which points to the

2. For just one example, Gregory of Nazianzus suggests that we know *that* the Son is begotten of the Father and *that* the Holy Spirit proceeds from the Father. However, we do not know precisely what is involved in the generation of the Son and the procession of the Spirit. See Gregory, "Fifth Theological Oration" 7–8 (Wickham, 121–22).

timelessness of God. And that distinction is important, but time is not the only point of difference between God and creation. All creatures are conditioned in a variety of ways—we have different (and limited) powers, for example. Physical creatures (leaving angels aside for the moment) exist in a particular place at any given moment of time. By contrast, God is unconditioned and limitless. The most important difference of all is that all creatures are contingent; that is, we are all dependent on God for our very existence. Christian theologians have long pointed out that this does not just mean God created us at the beginning, but also that God continually and actively wills the existence of all creation. But God alone is the cause of his own existence eternally. Once we begin to grasp that distinction, we can begin to recognize how futile it is for contingent and conditioned creatures to try to take in the fullness of the unconditioned and eternal source of all things.

The other reason is the effect of sin on our cognitive functioning. Even apart from the presence of sin, our finitude would keep us from comprehending God in his fullness. But sin has made the problem much deeper. The effects of sin are wide-ranging, of course, but the effect on our minds is not to be underestimated. Living in a fallen world—and furthering the world's brokenness through our own actions—has clouded our understanding and made it difficult to recognize the true, the good, and the beautiful. This is, in fact, a key theme in the New Testament, particularly in the letters of Paul. In Ephesians 4, for example, Paul contrasts his readers' former way of life with the way of Christ: "You must no longer walk as the gentiles walk, in the futility of their minds; they are darkened in their understanding, alienated from the life of God because of their ignorance and hardness of heart. They have lost all sensitivity and have abandoned themselves to licentiousness, greedy to practice every kind of impurity. That is not the way you learned Christ!" (4:17–20). Note here that the spiritual damage of sin and the compromised understanding are connected. Hardness of heart has eroded the capacity to discern the good, leading to more and more wayward practices. The remedy that Paul outlines for such a condition involves putting away the old self, being clothed with the new self, and being "renewed in the spirit of your minds" (4:23).

If Ephesians 4 captures the connection between compromised minds and compromised lives, then another Pauline text is even more direct in charting the effect of sin on our ability to know God. In 1 Corinthians 2, Paul explores the problem of human beings trying to discern the divine. Since only God can comprehend the depths of God, we are dependent upon the Spirit (who is God) to reveal to us what we know of God. "God has revealed to us through the Spirit, for the Spirit searches everything, even the depths of God. For what human knows what is truly human except the human spirit that is within? So also no one comprehends what is truly God's except the Spirit of God" (2:10–11). At first glance, it may appear that Paul is building a case here solely on the basis of human finitude. But he is clear that the world's rebellion against God has intensified the problem. Throughout the chapter, he contrasts the human wisdom of the "rulers of this age" with the wisdom that God has revealed (repeatedly in 2:4–8 and again in 2:12–15). There is an unmistakable moral culpability that Paul associates with the wisdom of this age, whose practitioners "are being destroyed" (2:6) and responded to divine wisdom by crucifying Christ (2:8). In fact, this First Corinthians text brings together the problem of finitude and the problem of sin to face squarely our inability to comprehend God. Yet the same text offers confidence in what God has graciously revealed to us: "'For who has known the mind of the Lord so as to instruct him?' But we have the mind of Christ" (2:16).

All of this suggests that we should approach theology with both a proper confidence and a proper humility. We can embrace the classic teaching of the Christian faith with confidence, because this teaching is rooted in God's gracious self-revelation and the Spirit-enabled reception of divine revelation in the community of faith. And yet in humility, we recognize that these teachings affirm the transcendence of the God who has reached out to us. In other words, as Augustine reminded us, we will not be able to comprehend the fullness of the God who has made himself known to us. The intersections of time and space with eternity, such as the resurrection appearances of Jesus, are to be welcomed and cherished. This is because they are markers of the divine activity that has made it possible, in God's grace, to draw us flesh-and-blood creatures into a share of eternity. But as we proceed in the work of theology, reflecting upon those encounters, we must never suppose that we can take full account of the boundless eternity of God. The apostle Paul's famous passage on love in 1 Corinthians 13 captures this well: "For we know only in part, and we prophesy only in part, but when the complete comes, the partial will come to an end . . . . For now we see only a reflection, as in a mirror, but then we will see face to face. Now I know only in part; then I will know fully, even as I have been fully known" (13:9–10, 12).

With this in mind, let us return to the Emmaus story. One way in which we can read the vanishing of Jesus is as a narrative reminder of God's boundless transcendence. The key to this reading is the timing of Jesus's disappearance: it happens right when the disciples recognize him. The disciples truly understand, finally, what has been revealed to them in the course of their journey and who it was that revealed it. But that does not mean that they know everything of God and God's purposes. Jesus was truly, bodily, at the table with them, but his presence was on his terms and in his timing. Any attempt to hold on to Jesus, to begin to inquire into the divine mysteries on the disciples' terms, is headed off by his vanishing. And despite the two disciples' slowness to understand early in the narrative, they seem to get this part right. There is not a hint of disappointment in their response to the disappearance of Jesus. On the contrary, they reflect joyfully on how Jesus had opened the Scriptures to them. In other words, they accept the terms of this revelatory encounter and do not show any inclination to demand more from Jesus. In that respect, their response is a good model for all of us who study theology. We can gratefully welcome and reflect on what God has revealed to us, even as we recognize that there is much that is not given to us to know.

So far, we have been considering the nature of the content of Christian theology. That is, our claims about God are trustworthy because they are rooted in divine revelation, but by no means do they exhaust the full mystery of God. Now we turn to explore the eschatological character of theology from a second perspective. Here we will ask where Christian theology points us, what difference it actually makes. There is no question that Christian theology, when it is approached rightly, makes a difference in our lives and in the world for the present. But I want to suggest that we too often neglect the most important impact of Christian teaching: that we can come to share, by grace, in God's eternity. Theology is ultimately faithful testimony to God's activity in drawing creation toward the eternal glorification of God.

To begin, we might clarify that eternity in this context does not simply mean a really long time. In other words, we are not just talking about the world as we know it continuing in an indefinitely extended future. Instead, we might think of eternity as the realm in which God simply is who he is, without beginning or end. The dimensions of time and space are a function of God's creation, and God himself transcends those dimensions. Eternity is the realm out of which time and space were made by God. This is one of those areas that is hard for us, as creatures living in time, to grasp in any fully satisfying sense. But it seems reasonable to suppose that the arena of time and space was given for God's creatures to be able to make choices—most fundamentally, the choice to respond to God's love with love for God and his creation.[3] The biblical narrative traces the ways that we have repeatedly chosen poorly, and yet it also conveys how God has continually reached out to us in grace to draw us back into right relationship. The work of Jesus for us and the work of the Holy Spirit in us enables the restoration of this right relationship. When we welcome that divine work of salvation, the relationship of loving and glorifying God will transcend even time itself.

---

3. C. S. Lewis's *The Great Divorce* remains a beautiful exploration of the role of time and space as the realm of an eternal choice that each of us makes.

The point of all this is to say that theology is not only about this life. The ultimate aim of God's saving work is not the present, or even our future within the bounds of time. The ultimate aim is that we may come to share in God's eternity, joining in the love and worship of God that will continue even when time has run its course. It is certainly true that we begin to share in the eternal life offered by Jesus now, in this life.[4] The life of each Christian and the activity of the community of faith serve as signs of God's eternal kingdom, right here in the realm of time and space. In that light, Christian theology does truly make a difference for this life. But it would be easy for a student reading some contemporary theology to get the impression that the only value of theology is the social, political, or economic impact it can make in our world in the present. The Christian faith does indeed help to orient our social and political lives in the present. But we must be clear. Christianity offers more than just a set of tools for shaping our world; it offers victory over death by the power of Jesus's resurrection. "If Christ has not been raised, your faith is futile, and you are still in your sins," writes the apostle Paul (1 Cor 15:17). He continues: "If for this life only we have hoped in Christ, we are of all people most to be pitied. But in fact Christ has been raised from the dead, the first fruits of those who have died" (15:19–20). The Christian faith stands or falls with the resurrection of Christ. Because Christ is indeed risen, Paul contends, our hope is not in vain—and that hope points us beyond this life.

I want to be careful not to give the impression that our hope for this world and our hope for the next are at odds. Rather, the point I am making is twofold. First, we cannot limit our focus to the impact of Christian theology for the present world alone. If we miss the promise of life beyond death, of all that awaits in the heavenly banquet, then we are missing the main course. We would be, as Paul suggests, of all people most to be pitied. Second, it is the hope of eternity that shapes our hope for the present, and not vice-versa. Here is where the language of signs (which

---

4. This is an important theme in the Gospel of John. See, for example, John 4:36; 5:24; and 17:3.

we used in the previous paragraph) becomes so important. Signs are not merely symbols; signs are symbols that participate in the reality signified. When Jesus did miracles during his earthly ministry, for example, each miracle was a sign of the kingdom of God breaking into a particular corner of our world. A physical healing or the driving out of a demon did not mean that suffering was thereby eliminated from the face of the earth. It did mean that Jesus was offering a sign, a window into the eternal kingdom where all suffering is wiped away.

I want to suggest that we should look at the active engagement of Christians in this world, which the study of theology rightly empowers, in just this way. We might consider the example of ecclesiastical abolitionists in the nineteenth century.[5] The efforts of these Christians toward the abolition of slavery—and the fruit of those efforts—are best understood as signs that point to God's eternal kingdom right in the midst of time and space. It would be a deep mistake to suppose that the main value of proclaiming the coming kingdom is in its effectiveness for resourcing temporal political goals. In fact, this would be to get matters backwards. Instead, the ultimate hope of Christians is in God's promise to heal all suffering and eliminate death itself in the world to come (Rev 21:1–4). The call for Christians to seek the good of their communities and the world in the present is right and necessary precisely to embody and signify this ultimate hope.

As we go about the study of theology, then, we should keep in mind that what Christians do and say in the public sphere must always be oriented by our eternal hope. And this claim carries another implication for our own formation as Christians. We are being prepared and built up by the Holy Spirit for eternity in God's presence. That is, the impact of theology is not only seen in what we communicate to the world or how we shape the world—though both of those are certainly part of it. The impact of theology is also seen in the kind of people we are becoming by God's grace. The reason that God calls us to impact the world around

5. Douglas M. Strong's *Perfectionist Politics* offers the definitive history of this movement and their theological motivations.

us is not because God somehow needs our help in bringing his will to fulfillment. Rather, God graciously invites us to live as signs of the eternal kingdom in order to align what God wants to do *in* us with what God wants to do *through* us. Given how deeply sin has marked our own lives as well as the world around us, we need more than marching orders: we need to become new people. The classic name for this process is sanctification, which refers to the Holy Spirit's work of transforming us according to the image of Christ. Only in and through this process can we be strengthened in our minds, hearts, and wills to stand in God's presence in the eternal kingdom.

While the power of sanctification comes from God, we do have a role to play in welcoming this power into our lives. We do this mainly by practicing the classic means of grace, such as praying, reading Scripture, worshiping, receiving the sacraments, and so on. Those practices are essential ways in which all Christians receive the Spirit's transformative work into their lives. But there is also a role for the study of theology to play in this process. It is certainly not the case that sanctification requires a formal degree in theology; most will never have the opportunity to pursue that path. For those who do study theology, though, their work can be a means that the Holy Spirit uses to renew and shape the mind. Indeed, Romans 12 suggests an important connection between this transformation of the mind and faithful action: "Do not be conformed to this age, but be transformed by the renewing of the mind, so that you may discern what is the will of God—what is good and acceptable and perfect" (12:2). It should be obvious that the study of theology can only play this role to the extent that it is pursued in a posture that is open to God's transformative work. But for those who approach theological reading, writing, and conversation in this spirit, it can be a means of preparation for the eternal joy of worshiping God in the life to come.

This preparation of our lives for eternity, in fact, offers us a second way of understanding the vanishing of Jesus in the Emmaus story. We noted above that we can read Jesus's disappearance as a reminder of God's transcendence. But we also find sprinkled throughout the Christian tradition another suggestion: that the very different way Jesus relates to his disciples after the resurrection enables their own transformation. We see it, for instance, in the commentary on the Gospel of Luke by the fifth-century bishop and theologian Cyril of Alexandria. Commenting on the disappearance from the Emmaus table, he suggests that the new phase of Jesus's relationship to his disciples enables their preparation for union with the incorruptible God: "For our Lord's relation unto men after his resurrection does not continue the same as before, for they too have need of renovation, and a second life in Christ, that the renewed may associate with the renewed, and the incorruptible approach the incorruptible."[6] Notably, Cyril immediately connects this point to Mary Magdalene's encounter with Jesus outside the tomb in John 20. "For which reason, as John tells us, He did not permit Mary to touch him, until He should go away and return again."[7] Granted, this is a rather cryptic comment on a rather cryptic moment in John's Gospel. But Cyril's point seems to be that the withdrawal of the kind of direct physical interaction Jesus shared with his disciples during his earthly ministry begins to enable their own movement toward incorruptibility in eternity.

Cyril's suggestion points to a kind of spiritual physics, in that the risen Jesus is leading the way on a journey we will all take toward a different plane of bodily existence in eternity. This idea is echoed by the medieval bishop and theologian St. Bonaventure in his commentary on Luke. Bonaventure emphasizes the role of Jesus's disappearance in shaping the desire of the disciples to relate to Jesus in a new manner going forward. Reflecting on Jesus's vanishing at Emmaus, he writes: "For by removing the corporal presence a desire for the spiritual presence is sparked and is enkindled by a remembrance of Christ."[8] His point seems to be that if Jesus were to remain with them in the manner of immediate physical presence, as at the Emmaus table, then the disciples might be content to remain as they were. But the withdrawal of

6. Cyril, *Commentary on the Gospel of St. Luke*, 617.
7. Cyril, *Commentary on the Gospel of St. Luke*, 617.
8. Bonaventure, *Commentary on the Gospel of Luke*, 2224.

that physical presence brought forth a hunger to relate to the risen Jesus in a new way. And the new manner of experiencing Jesus's presence requires the Spirit's work of transformation within the disciples. In other words, sanctification prepares the disciples to continue to be in the presence of Jesus, even eternally. Drawing from Bonaventure, then, we can read the disappearance of Jesus as a call to sanctification, which will enable us to join Jesus at the table of the heavenly banquet.

In this regard, the vanishing at Emmaus functions as an anticipation of the ascension. When Jesus ascends to the right hand of God the Father in heaven (Luke 24:50–52; Acts 1:6–11), he withdraws one kind of physical presence to enable another kind of presence with his disciples. That is, Jesus is no longer present to the disciples only at one place and time but will now be present with them in all places and times (Matt 28:20).[9] After Jesus's ascension, his followers are being prepared by the Spirit to join in the eternal feast of the kingdom. In this light, the appearances of the risen Jesus to the disciples before the ascension play a very specific role. No doubt, the resurrection appearances are crucial for confirming God's victory over death and for the commissioning of the disciples to serve as Jesus's witnesses. But if we take Bonaventure's reflections on the Emmaus story seriously, these appearances also stir the disciples' hunger for deeper communion with Jesus. Their encounters with the risen Jesus serve as a transition from how they knew him during his ministry to how they will know him eternally. Perhaps this helps us to understand why the disciples at Emmaus expressed no regret that Jesus had vanished, for their time at the table with him had by no means come to an end.

In order to move forward in their journey to dine with Jesus eternally, they would need the company of his other disciples. And this leads us to one last surprise in the Emmaus narrative. Even though night has arrived in Emmaus, the two disciples do not remain hunkered down in the safety of the place where they ate with Jesus. Their seeming astonishment at the recognition of

9. Churches that affirm the real presence of Christ in the Eucharist will, of course, understand this as a bodily as well as a spiritual presence.

Jesus, and his subsequent disappearance, stirs them to action. They immediately head back out on the road to Jerusalem to seek out the eleven apostles and their companions (Luke 24:33).[10] They are, without a doubt, excited to share with the others their account of their experience along the road and at the table. But we should also recognize in this movement a proper instinct; namely, to be in the company of the community of faith. The encounter with the risen Jesus had left them hungry to join the presence of his other followers. When we have had a deep and powerful experience of the Lord's presence, our desire for even deeper communion with him leads us to the fellowship of other Christians. It is this instinct that we will explore in our final chapter.

10. We should keep in mind that the Emmaus encounter happened before Matthias was chosen to replace Judas among the apostles (Acts 1:15–26), so there were only eleven apostles at the time.

Chapter 7: **The Return to Jerusalem**

THE TWO DISCIPLES OF the Emmaus story are not initially cast in a very favorable light. When the risen Jesus meets them on the road, they are visibly sad. This is in spite of the fact that they have heard a report of Jesus's empty tomb and the claim of angels that he is alive—news that should have brought them considerable hope. Jesus himself confirms their lack of faith by scolding their foolishness and slowness to believe (Luke 24:25–26). But as the story proceeds, the portrait of these two disciples gradually becomes more positive. It seems that spending time in Jesus's presence draws them from despair to joy. They beg Jesus to stay with them at Emmaus, and he accepts their invitation. As we saw in the last chapter, they do not show a hint of disappointment or anger when Jesus vanishes. In other words, they appear to hit every right note as the narrative draws to a close.

One final reaction by these disciples also seems to be commended by the text. After recognizing Jesus, who has now disappeared, the disciples do not hunker down in the safety of the place they are staying. Rather, "that same hour" they head out into the darkness of the night and make their way toward Jerusalem (v. 33). Their purpose is to connect with the other followers of Jesus: "They found the eleven and their companions gathered together." The disciples at Jerusalem report to the travelers that Jesus is alive and that he has appeared to Simon. In response, the two disciples tell the gathered company about the Emmaus road experience. Their

CHAPTER 7: THE RETURN TO JERUSALEM

instinct to connect with the broader fellowship of Jesus's followers signals a final guideline for Christian theology: *The proper home for theology is the community of faith. It is always to be carried out in conversation with and accountability to the church across the ages.*

Granted, this way of talking strikes us as somewhat odd in the modern world. For one thing, we tend to think of the proper home of theology as the university because it is an academic discipline. And there is something right about this, since academic institutions such as universities and seminaries offer very helpful resources for our studies. We benefit from libraries, from the expertise of professors, and from the discipline and rigor that academic life requires. Yet as we have seen throughout this book, the subject matter of theology is the Christian community's testimony to God's nature and activity. We can and should use the tools of the academy to go about our theological work, but ultimately it is the church's faith that is at the heart of that work. In this light, it is worth remembering that the earliest Christian theologians tended to be bishops. Their oversight of the church included the crucial role of articulating and teaching the faith. Even as the work of theology expanded to monasteries and eventually to universities, the shared commitments of the community of faith remained—and indeed they must remain—at the center of this work.

Another reason that the communal context of theology might strike us as strange is the modern tendency to highlight the innovation and creativity of individual theologians. The praise given to books and authors in theology (such as it is) often emphasizes edginess or the breaking of boundaries. Students in theology can quickly get the impression that the great sin in our discipline is to repeat what has been said before without offering anything new. But I want to suggest that this preoccupation with innovation is, historically speaking, a relatively recent development. And it can mislead us as to the nature of our task. Remember that the basis of our claims in Christian theology is God's self-revelation as received faithfully by the Christian community. To the degree that innovation moves outside what has been passed down to us by that community across the centuries, it is leading us off course.

One person who understood this especially well was the Methodist theologian Thomas C. Oden. In his memoir *Change of Heart*, he describes a curious experience. The experience happened shortly after Oden had made a major change of direction in his career (a shift that gave his book its title). At the prompting of a colleague at Drew University, the philosopher Will Herberg, Oden had begun to delve deeply into the classic texts of the Christian tradition.[1] As he moved down this path, he felt he was truly encountering the richness and brilliance of the tradition for the first time. Then he had a dream. "In the season of Epiphany 1971 I had a curious dream in which I was in the New Haven cemetery and accidentally stumbled upon my own tombstone with this puzzling epitaph: 'He made no new contribution to theology.'" While many contemporary theologians would see this as a mark of failure, Oden's response was the opposite: "I woke up refreshed and relieved."[2] Why would he feel this way?

Oden recalled that his graduate training had taught him that the most important task of the theologian was to think creatively and make a new contribution. "Nothing . . . was drummed into my head more steadily than the aspiration that the theology I would seek would be my own and my uniqueness would imprint it."[3] But now he had come to realize that this training had sent him in the wrong direction. He had discovered that early Christian writers, Irenaeus in particular, deplored the notion of innovation in theology. "What the ancient church teachers least wished for Christian teachers is that they would become focused on self-expression or become an assertion of purely private inspiration, as if those might claim to be some decisive improvement on apostolic teaching."[4]

---

1. Oden describes the decisive encounter with Herberg in *Change of Heart*, 136–37. Though it may seem odd that a theologian well into his career had not become well acquainted with these texts, his training and early scholarly work focused primarily on contemporary sources. One of the main themes in Oden's memoir is his regret that this pattern is all too common in theological education.

2. Oden, *Change of Heart*, 143.

3. Oden, *Change of Heart*, 144.

4. Oden, *Change of Heart*, 144.

From that point on, Oden set out to work as a theologian within the great tradition that had been passed down through the ages and "to abstain from creating any new doctrine." He concludes, "It was the best decision I had made as a theologian."[5] It must be noted that the rest of Oden's career as a theologian was deeply influential—there is no doubt that he made a significant contribution to theology, even if it was not a new one. Given his testimony, we can conclude that this contribution was made possible by his faithfulness to the tradition rather than any desire for self-expression.

None of this is to say that there isn't room for creativity in Christian theology. In fact, the best theological minds are those that have the capacity to think in fresh ways *with* and *within* the great tradition. Language and cultural patterns are continually evolving, so an ongoing task of the theologian is to build bridges between the Christian tradition and the familiar ways of thinking in a given time and place. But one is only in a position to do this if one has been deeply immersed in the historic church's life and teaching. The first goal of the theologian is not to find something new to say but rather to listen to and understand what has been taught and passed on to us. Then one will be able to work prayerfully to generate fresh and creative expressions of Christian teaching for each generation.

It is for this reason that I would caution you about a way of talking that has become quite common in recent years. More and more we hear references to "my theology" or "your theology" or even "theologies" in the plural. And, to be fair, this is not entirely new—even old hands will find references to "Schleiermacher's theology" or "Barth's theology" to be familiar. But we should notice what is happening in this pattern of speaking: theology does not here refer to a discipline of reflection within a shared tradition, but rather to the *product* of reflection. (To get a sense for what has happened, imagine a professor of biology or psychology encouraging a class of new students to develop their own biologies or psychologies.) My point here is not to scold people for talking that way so much as to suggest that it reflects the preoccupation with

5. Oden, *Change of Heart*, 144.

the new that has characterized contemporary theology. In such a setting, one wonders if the desire to establish the uniqueness of "my" theology ultimately reveals an understanding of theology as glorified self-expression. By contrast, a more classical understanding of theology envisions shared reflection on the treasures that have been given to the community of faith by means of divine revelation. We get a glimpse of an early form of this practice in the reunited disciples at Jerusalem, as they shared how Jesus had been made known to them (Luke 24:34–35).

The raw material that the theologian works with, therefore, is the common teaching of the church through time and space. Our next point should then be rather obvious: to be faithful in that work, the theologian must be shaped by the life of the church. This formation happens in a number of ways. Reading is an especially important one for the theologian in particular. We must be clear, of course, that one does not need to be literate to be a faithful Christian formed by the church (many Christians in late antiquity and in the medieval era could not read or write). But the particular vocation of theology within the life of the church requires reading deeply and widely. As we saw in chapter 3, the Bible should be at the center of the theologian's regular habit of reading. And given all that we said above, we need to acquaint ourselves with the way that Scripture has been received in the community of faith over the generations. That means that studying theology also involves reading the great works that have endured by shaping Christian thought and life. When one is starting out, it can be daunting to try to figure out where to begin in this task. This is one reason why it is helpful to have formal programs of study, in which experts can guide students through a variety of classic works that are intellectually and spiritually profitable. And while theology inevitably involves reading actual books, at its best it will also involve reading of a wider sort—including Christian art, hymns, architecture, and other material bearers of the Christian tradition.

In previous chapters, we have explored other practices by which theologians are shaped by life in the church. Chapter 5, for example, examined the importance of participating in Christian worship for the practice of sound theology. The essential connection between prayer and theology, furthermore, was considered at length in chapter 2. These practices are typically known as spiritual disciplines; that is, they are activities through which the Holy Spirit shapes us in the likeness of Christ.[6] Even though there is no fixed or formal list of spiritual disciplines in the Christian tradition, many of them have long been recognized as deeply transformative. The Spirit works powerfully through these practices to shape our hearts, minds, and wills. Along with reading Scripture, worship, and prayer, we might point to receiving the sacraments, fasting, confession, silence, and acts of service and charity as examples of recognized spiritual disciplines.

A crucial point to understand, particularly for the purposes of this chapter, is that the spiritual disciplines are gifts that God has given us *through the church*. It is true, of course, that we can practice certain spiritual disciplines on our own. But we learn *how* to pray, to fast, to worship, and so on—as well as *why* these practices are so important—by active participation in the community of faith. Even private prayer or reading Scripture on our own are gifts that come from God through the community of faith. This point becomes even more clear when we practice spiritual disciplines together: worshiping together, praying together, receiving the sacraments, and the like. When the Holy Spirit forms us through our participation in these disciplines, the Spirit is working through the life of the community. There is no doubt that this transformation impacts the way we do our work as theologians. The theologian can only give public expression to the faith of the church to the extent that the theologian is shaped by the practices that form the members of that church.

So far, we have been focused primarily on activities such as reading and practicing the spiritual disciplines as ways that life in the church shapes the theologian. But there is also an important dimension of fellowship within the community of faith that is

6. There are a number of very helpful introductions to the spiritual disciplines, including Richard Foster's *Celebration of Discipline*, April Yamasaki's *Sacred Pauses*, and Dallas Willard's *The Spirit of the Disciplines*.

necessary for faithful theology. This appears to be at work at the end of the Emmaus story. We are not explicitly told why the two disciples travel in the dark from Emmaus to Jerusalem. Presumably, the impulse to share the news of their encounter with the risen Jesus is part of it, since this is just what they do in verse 35. But one also gets the sense that they simply longed to be with the other disciples. Their first action upon reaching Jerusalem is to find the eleven apostles and their companions, who are gathered together (v. 33). From then to now, theologians do their work out of the fellowship they share with other followers of Jesus.

I want to emphasize three aspects of communal fellowship that are essential to the work of theology: mutual encouragement, accountability, and the sharing of joys and burdens. Granted, none of these are unique to theologians—they are part of what it means to be an active participant in the church for any Christian. But precisely because they are concrete means of fellowship with the community of faith, these aspects must form the theologian who speaks out of the shared life and teaching of the church. The New Testament is brimming with calls to this kind of fellowship. Mutual encouragement is beautifully described in Hebrews 10:24–25: "And let us consider how to provoke one another to love and good deeds, not neglecting to meet together, as is the habit of some, but encouraging one another, and all the more as you see the Day approaching." More succinctly, Paul exhorts readers in 1 Thessalonians to "encourage one another and build up each other" (5:11).

Yet these positive words of mutual encouragement go hand-in-hand with honest accountability. The fellowship within the community of faith is aimed at welcoming the Spirit's work of transformation, and thus truth-telling in love is sometimes necessary. Colossians 3:16, for example, includes the call to "teach and admonish one another in all wisdom." It must be noted, of course, that this exhortation follows repeated appeals to love and mercy: "Clothe yourselves with compassion, kindness, humility, meekness, and patience. Bear with one another and, if anyone has a complaint against another, forgive each other; just as the Lord has forgiven you, so you must also forgive. Above all, clothe yourselves with love, which binds everything together in perfect harmony" (Col 3:12–14). Similarly, in 1 Thessalonians 5, Paul's appeal to mutual accountability is held together with an insistence on encouragement and patience: "And we urge you, brothers and sisters, to admonish the idlers, encourage the fainthearted, help the weak, be patient with all of them" (5:14). The combination of patience, accountability, and encouragement in this passage offers an important reminder. Whenever we consider the place of accountability within the fellowship of the church, we need to be careful to specify the context. The work of sharing honestly about places in our lives that need attention is best done in settings where there are established relationships in place, particularly relationships where such accountability has been invited. A great example is a standing small group, where group members know each other well and are mutually committed to relationships of accountability. These types of small groups can bring tremendous spiritual growth when Christians participate honestly, openly, and consistently.

Another aspect of fellowship that is essential for Christian community—and thus for faithful theology—is the sharing of joys and burdens. Again, we see this emphasis in the New Testament letters. First Corinthians 12, for example, envisions the church as the body of Christ, in which there is a kind of reversal of expectations. Parts of the body—that is, members of the church's fellowship—that might be thought of as weaker or less honorable are in fact to be treated with greater respect and honor (12:22–24). God has so arranged the body of fellowship in this way, the apostle Paul continues, "that there may be no dissention within the body, but the members may have the same care for one another. If one member suffers, all suffer together with it; if one member is honored, all rejoice together with it" (12:25–26). The image of the body here is particularly helpful in capturing this mutual shared life in the fellowship of the church—to separate one part of the body from the rest would make it useless. In a similar way, for any members of the community to separate themselves from the joys and burdens of others would effectively be to render useless the gifts God has given to serve and build up the community. A similar picture is drawn in Galatians 6:2: "Bear one another's burdens, and in this way you will fulfill the law of Christ." The immediately preceding verse may suggest that the burdens Paul has in mind are fellow believers' struggles against particular sins, which would offer further testimony to the point that accountability belongs within relationships of love and sharing.[7] In any case, the call to bear each other's burdens makes it clear that members of the community of Christ's disciples are to walk with each other through the good and the bad.

How, then, do these various dimensions of Christian fellowship shape the particular work of theology? It is certainly the case, as we emphasized in chapter 1, that theology begins with the testimony of the church to God's activity rather than with the theologian's own experience. But it is also the case that the church's proclamation is aimed at drawing actual people into communion with God. And it is simply not possible for the theologian to articulate the church's teaching faithfully without experience of that teaching as it is embodied in the actual life of the church. The journey of discipleship, marked by mutual encouragement, accountability, and the sharing of joys and burdens, is where we see lives actually changed. If a theologian is not walking that road in the company of other disciples, then a crucial part of the picture is missed. Looking across the Christian tradition, some of the most insightful theologians—think of St. Augustine, St. Gregory the Great, or John Wesley—have drawn upon their own pastoral experience to articulate the common teaching of the church across the ages. A theologian does not need to be a pastor, of course, but a theologian does need to be in fellowship with the community of faith to understand how the church's teaching takes root in actual lives. Books are central to our work, but an understanding of the Christian faith drawn only from books will be insufficient.

7. Given Paul's rather staccato and succinct style at the beginning of Galatians 6, it is also possible that the point about bearing each other's burdens in verse 2 is distinct from the point about transgressions and accountability in verse 1.

Not only does a theologian's understanding of the faith need to be drawn from actual life in the church, but also the fruit of the theologian's work needs to be offered to the community of faith. This takes us to our next major point: The labors of theology are primarily directed toward the good of the life of the church, not toward the academy. Christian theology is a vocation of the church, and what emerges from that work is ultimately for the church. Having said that, we need immediately to head off a couple of potential misunderstandings. The first has to do with the audience that professional theologians address. It would be a mistake to suppose that theologians should only write for general audiences and never for professional academic audiences. While the yield of theology is ultimately intended for the community of faith, professional guilds play an important role in refining that work. The critical questions, cross-disciplinary insights, and unexpected connections that emerge from academic exchanges often improve the precision, historical accuracy, and clarity of theological claims. I do think it is a good and healthy practice for professional theologians to write regularly for general audiences. Addressing Christians who are trying to live out their faith amidst the challenges of work and family life helps the professional to speak with greater directness and clarity, qualities that academic training does not always cultivate. At the same time, it is important for theologians to bring their work before other professionals who will evaluate their work with critical rigor.

A second potential misunderstanding follows naturally from the first. To say that theology is for the church is not to say that theologians should avoid highly technical work. There is no getting around the fact that Christian teaching goes quite deep in many areas, most centrally in addressing the nature of the God who has revealed himself to us as triune. It is true that we can offer summaries of Christian doctrine that help initiate new Christians into the faith. Many people in the church will never have reason to explore the intricacies of the relations among the persons of the Trinity or the communication of attributes in Christology. But details such as these are still part of the historic teaching of the Christian faith, and for the theologian, it is important to engage them. In fact, expertise in technical theological matters is particularly important when difficult questions arise in the life of the church. It is often the case, historically speaking, that similar questions gave rise to the kind of technical precision we see in the great theological works of the Christian tradition. So it is important in every generation to have people within the community of faith with facility in these areas to address questions as faithfully and truthfully as possible. To put the matter very directly, theology done for the church does not mean producing a watered-down version of Christian teaching.

With those words of caution in mind, we are in a position to specify what it does mean to say that the fruit of theology is ultimately for the church. First, it means that the work of theology is aimed at guiding the preaching and worship of the church. Ideally, this happens both at the macro level and at the micro level. At the macro level, denominations draw upon the work of theologians as they consider proposed revisions to their major doctrinal statements (these documents have various names depending on the denomination—articles of religion, confessions of faith, statements of faith, and the like). And we saw in chapter 5 how theologians are typically involved in the development and revision of liturgies and worship resources for the various churches. At the micro level, the guidance and teaching that pastors offer to congregations is significantly shaped by the work of theology. Some of this happens in the educational training of ministers, whether in a seminary program or through some other form of preparation for ministry. But some of this is ongoing, as pastors continue to read and engage the work of theologians (and here I mean the term to include Bible scholars, church historians, liturgical scholars, and other experts). Obviously, the degree to which ministers actually do this varies—those with good training tend to continue growing in their theological education throughout their lives in ministry. It is not too much to say that the health of the church's teaching at the local level of the congregation depends on the degree to which pastors continue to draw upon the theological resources available to them.

Second, to say that theology is ultimately for the church means that theologians will be attentive to questions emerging out of the actual life of faith. This reinforces what we said above about the importance of theologians remaining within the fellowship of the community of faith. It is in the context of this fellowship that theologians get a direct sense of areas where people are struggling or pondering particular questions. And it should go without saying that these struggles and questions may emerge from the theologians' own experience, not just from the experience of those with whom they are walking. I would add that it is a good practice for professional theologians to be in regular contact with pastors and other church leaders to hear their perspectives on where theological attention is needed. Academic theologians often emphasize that church leadership needs the work that emerges from seminaries and universities, but it also works in the other direction: theologians need the insights of church leaders to do their work well. None of this means, of course, that the everyday experience of Christians determines the *content* of Christian doctrine. It does mean that those who teach Christian doctrine must be attentive to that everyday experience in order to understand *how* to teach and write well.

We have been focused in the preceding paragraphs on the work of professional theologians, but it is also true that the work of students in theology serves the good of the church. This happens in a number of ways. First, from a long-term perspective, students in theology programs are preparing to serve the community of faith in ways that align with their particular gifts and callings. For some, this will mean pastoral ministry. For others, it will mean some other form of service to the church (whether they are employed by a congregation or not). For all, a good theological education will equip students with the resources to put their gifts to use for the benefit of the body of Christ. Second, many if not most theology students are already active in some form of ministry in their congregations as they go about their studies. Internships are one formal way in which this happens, but many students already offer some form of congregational leadership quite apart from an official internship. These ministry settings can provide very helpful experience in drawing upon the riches of the Christian tradition that students are learning about in the classroom to serve the nuts-and-bolts work of the church. Finally, students serve the church indirectly through their contributions *in* the classrooms and hallways of their theology programs. Their questions, comments, and insights often enhance the understanding of their professors and fellow students—which, in turn, positively impacts the communities that those people serve.

I want to conclude this chapter, and indeed the book, with one final point that relates to the community of disciples in Jerusalem. While much of the action of the Emmaus story takes place on the road, and while the climax of the story takes place at the table in the village of Emmaus, the story actually ends in Jerusalem. And the story that follows it in the Gospel of Luke is significant: While the two disciples from the Emmaus road are talking with the others in Jerusalem, the risen Jesus makes another appearance beginning in verse 36. The connecting point between these two narratives in the last chapter of Luke is the gathered community of the followers of Jesus. And it is to the complete community of disciples that Jesus finally appears in a manner that is recognized by all of them (vv. 36–49).[8] (It is true that, while they immediately recognize Jesus as Jesus in this latter story, they wonder for quite a while if they are seeing a ghost. Jesus responds by allowing them to touch him and by eating a piece of fish in front of them to assure them that he is bodily present to them.)

If we recall that theology is ultimately meant to draw us toward God—a point that has been made throughout this book—then the manner in which Jesus appears to the disciples is significant. That is, the risen Jesus ultimately reveals himself *to the community gathered together*. The two disciples had experienced a transformative encounter with the risen Jesus along the road, but they hadn't recognized him until the very moment he vanished. Their response is to get up at that very hour and find

---

8. We do read indirectly in verse 34 about Jesus's appearance to Simon, but the first appearance in Luke of the risen Jesus (recognized by the disciples as Jesus) that is directly narrated is this story in verses 36–49.

the larger community of Jesus's followers. And it is there, with the other disciples, that they are able to spend time in Jesus's presence knowing who he is. During that time with Jesus, he prepares them for what is to come. And in the course of that conversation, Jesus does two things that should catch our attention.

The first, in Luke 24:45, is that "he opened their minds to understand the Scriptures." They now are able to see how Jesus had fulfilled the role of the messiah, as foretold by the prophets— the very thing the two disciples on the Emmaus road had been unable to grasp at first. The second thing Jesus does is to offer the disciples a final charge: "Repentance and forgiveness of sins is to be proclaimed in his name to all nations, beginning from Jerusalem. You are witnesses of these things" (24:47–48). We are right to read these two actions of Jesus—opening their minds to understand the Scriptures and commissioning them as his witnesses—as being connected. It is in the context of the apostolic community of faith, the very community that proclaims repentance and forgiveness of sins, that the Scriptures are interpreted. And Jesus makes it clear that they would not be fulfilling this call in their own power but rather in the power of the Holy Spirit that God the Father had promised and that Jesus would send at Pentecost (Luke 24:49; Acts 1:8; 2:1–4). Empowered by the Spirit, the journey of this community was just beginning.

In many ways, your journey is just beginning as well. As you proceed in your study of Christian theology, keep in mind that you do not fulfill God's call in your own power either. Like the disciples commissioned directly by the risen Jesus, you will serve as his witnesses in the power of the Holy Spirit. As you do so, remember the lessons from the Emmaus story that we have explored together. And remember the very last words of the Emmaus narrative, which offer a summary of the report the two disciples gave to the gathered community at Jerusalem. That report describes their conversation with Jesus along the road and the breaking of the bread, where Jesus had been made known to them. As you continue your journey in theology, my prayer is that Jesus will likewise be made known to you and, indeed, to all of us.

Bibliography

Augustine. *Confessions*. Translated by Henry Chadwick. Oxford: Oxford University Press, 1991.

———. *Sermons on the New Testament 94A–147A*. Vol. 3.4 of *The Works of Saint Augustine*. Translated by Edmund Hill. Brooklyn: New City, 1992.

Basil the Great. *On the Holy Spirit*. Translated by Stephen Hildebrand. Yonkers, NY: St. Vladimir's Seminary Press, 2011.

Benedict XVI. *From the Baptism in the Jordan to the Transfiguration*. Vol. 1 of *Jesus of Nazareth*. Translated by Adrian J. Walker. New York: Image, 2007.

Bonaventure. *Commentary on the Gospel of Luke*. Vol. 8.3 of *Works of St. Bonaventure*. Translated by Robert J. Karris. St. Bonaventure, NY: Franciscan Institute, 2004.

Book of Catechisms: Reference Edition. Louisville, KY: Geneva, 2001.

Buechner, Frederick. *Now and Then: A Memoir of Vocation*. San Francisco: HarperSanFrancisco, 1983.

———. *The Sacred Journey: A Memoir of Early Days*. San Francisco: HarperSanFrancisco, 1982.

Catechism of the Catholic Church. New York: Doubleday, 1995.

Catherine of Siena. *The Dialogue*. Translated by Suzanne Noffke. New York: Paulist, 1980.

Cyril of Alexandria. *Commentary on the Gospel of St. Luke*. Translated by R. Payne Smith. United States: Studion, 1983.

Evagrius Ponticus. "Chapters on Prayer." In *Evagrius Ponticus*, 185–201. Translated by A. M. Casiday. London: Routledge, 2006.

Foster, Richard J. *Celebration of Discipline: The Path to Spiritual Growth*. New York: HarperOne, 1998.

Gregory of Nazianzus. "The Fifth Theological Oration (Oration 31): On the Holy Spirit." In *On God and Christ: The Five Theological Orations and Two Letters to Cledonius*, 117–47. Translated by Lionel Wickham. Crestwood, NY: St. Vladimir's Seminary Press, 2002.

Julian of Norwich. *Revelations of Divine Love*. Translated by Elizabeth Spearing. London: Penguin, 1998.

Koskela, Douglas M. "The Authority of Scripture in its Ecclesial Context." In *Canonical Theism: A Proposal for Theology and the Church*, edited by William J. Abraham et al., 210–23. Grand Rapids: Eerdmans, 2008.

———. *The Radiance of God: Christian Doctrine Through the Image of Divine Light*. Eugene, OR: Cascade, 2021.

———. "What Is Love?" *Firebrand Magazine*, December 19, 2023. https://firebrandmag.com/articles/what-is-love.

Lawrence, Brother. *The Practice of the Presence of God*. Translated by Robert J. Edmonson. Orleans, MA: Paraclete, 1985.

Leith, John H., ed. *Creeds of the Churches: A Reader in Christian Doctrine from the Bible to the Present*. Louisville, KY: Westminster John Knox, 1982.

Lewis, C. S. *The Great Divorce*. New York: HarperOne, 1946.

———. "Preface." In *On the Incarnation*, by St. Athanasius, 9–16. Translated by John Behr. Yonkers, NY: St. Vladimir's Seminary Press, 2011.

Moser, Paul K. *The Elusive God: Reorienting Religious Epistemology*. Cambridge: Cambridge University Press, 2008.

Oden, Thomas C. *Change of Heart: A Personal and Theological Memoir*. Downers Grove, IL: IVP Academic, 2014.

Origen. *On First Principles*. Vol. 2. Translated by John Behr. Oxford: Oxford University Press, 2017.

Pelikan, Jaroslav. *The Emergence of the Catholic Tradition (100–600)*. Vol. 1 of *The Christian Tradition: A History of the Development of Doctrine*. Chicago: University of Chicago Press, 1971.

Schmemann, Alexander. *For the Life of the World: Sacraments and Orthodoxy*. Crestwood, NY: St. Vladimir's Seminary Press, 1973.

Strong, Douglas M. *Perfectionist Politics: Abolitionism and the Religious Tensions of American Democracy*. Syracuse, NY: Syracuse University Press, 1999.

Wainwright, Geoffrey. *Doxology: The Praise of God in Worship, Doctrine, and Life: A Systematic Theology*. Oxford: Oxford University Press, 1984.

———. *For Our Salvation: Two Approaches to the Work of Christ*. Grand Rapids: Eerdmans, 1997.

Wilken, Robert Louis. *The Spirit of Early Christian Thought: Seeking the Face of God*. New Haven: Yale University Press, 2003.

Willard, Dallas. *The Spirit of the Disciplines: Understanding How God Changes Lives*. San Francisco: Harper & Row, 1988.

Wright, Tom. *How God Became King: Getting to the Heart of the Gospels*. London: SPCK, 2012.

Yamasaki, April. *Sacred Pauses: Spiritual Practices for Personal Renewal*. Waterloo, ON: Herald, 2013.

www.ingramcontent.com/pod-product-compliance
Lightning Source LLC
Chambersburg PA
CBHW020208090426
42734CB00008B/980